W9-CFL-158

THE MOTHER GOD MADE ME TO BE

My Journey
from Newlywed,
to Mother of Two,
to Single Mom
Trying to Heal
and Become

THE MOTHER GOD MADE ME TO BE

KAREN VALENTIN

New York Nashville

Copyright © 2016 by Karen Valentin
Reading group guide copyright © 2016 by Hachette Book Group, Inc.

Cover design by Julee Brand
Cover copyright © 2016 by Hachette Book Group, Inc.

FaithWords
Hachette Book Group
1290 Avenue of the Americas
New York, NY 10104
faithwords.com
twitter.com/faithwords

First Edition: March 2016

FaithWords is a division of Hachette Book Group, Inc.
The FaithWords name and logo are trademarks of Hachette Book Group, Inc.

The publisher is not responsible for websites (or their content) that are not owned by the publisher.

The Hachette Speakers Bureau provides a wide range of authors for speaking events. To find out more, go to www.hachettespeakersbureau.com or call (866) 376-6591.

Unless otherwise indicated, Scripture quotations are taken from the New International Version of the Bible. Holy Bible, New International Version©, NIV©, Copyright ©1973, 1978, 1984, 2011 by Biblica, Inc. © Used by permission. All rights reserved worldwide.

Library of Congress Cataloging-in-Publication Data has been applied for.

ISBNs: 978-1-4555-3986-4 (hardcover), 978-1-4555-3985-7 (ebook),

Printed in the United States of America

RRD-C

10 9 8 7 6 5 4 3 2 1

For every mom who lets go of her pain,
to better carry her child.

CONTENTS

ACKNOWLEDGMENTS

With tremendous gratitude to:

My family and friends, who have loved me through it all.

Pastor Taylor Field and my co-workers at Graffiti Church, who showed me the kind of woman I want to become.

Adrienne Ingrum, whose friendship and mentoring for over ten years has changed my life. Thank you for believing in my voice and giving it a place to live.

My sons, Brandon and Tyler, the greatest love, joy, and inspiration in my life.

NEWLYWED

"It was a beautiful day, perfect for a wedding."

CROSSROADS

Why do you want to marry me?" my fiancé asked. I gripped the phone tighter and almost lost my breath. It was the morning of our wedding. My hair was in curlers, my white dress hung on the door, and my family bustled about in my sister's house, getting ready for the big event.

I stepped outside with the phone. It was a beautiful day, perfect for a wedding. "Why are you asking me that, Gavin?"

His response sent a wave of nausea through my body. "I'm at a crossroads here," he said.

My sister Diane poked her head out.

"Lisa's ready to do your hair."

"One sec," I said, waving her off as I walked farther away from the door. I tried to speak into the phone, but I paused. I felt like a game show contestant ready to lose a million dollars and a trip to Tahiti if I gave the wrong answer. But this was my life on the line—the life I'd envisioned with him.

"What are you doing to me? How dare you! How dare you do this to me right now!" That's what I really wanted to say, but I was the one who didn't dare.

"Because," I said, "I can't imagine my life without you in it. I see my future in you, I can see our kids we'll have one day in you, and because I love you. That's why."

He said a quiet "Okay," and I hung up the phone not knowing if he'd show up that day.

I held it in. I didn't tell a soul. I let my thoughts swirl around inside like a growing storm as everyone around me lit up, growing in their excitement for the wedding. We piled into cars to head over to the venue.

I should call off the wedding even if he does *show up,* I thought as I sat in the back of the car, looking blankly at the cloudless sky. *This is no way to start a marriage.*

We arrived and everything was lovely. Delicate flowers of cream and wine adorned each table. Just outside, the veranda was beautifully decorated, and the arch where we were to exchange our vows was covered in lilies. I willed my tears not to come.

"Isn't it so pretty," my mother said, taking it all in.

"Yes." I smiled.

Diane was holding the large garment bag with my dress inside.

"Let's go upstairs," she said. "You don't want Gavin to see you before the ceremony."

My sister and mother walked me into the bridal room. Champagne and cheese and fruit platters covered a small table. My oldest sister, Tilza, who had driven in from Vermont, burst through the door in excitement.

"There she is," she gushed, hugging me tight. "You already look so beautiful!"

Little by little the room filled. As each of my loved ones entered, there was an outpouring of love for me. Their sweet affection weighed on my heart as I imagined their joyful faces transformed into pity.

Gavin's sister peeked her head through the door. "We're here," she squealed. "Are you guys almost ready?"

The noise and bustle in the room seemed to stop as I focused only on her.

"He's here?"

"Yeah, he rode with us," she said casually between a kiss and hug for my mother.

All the tension in my shoulders relaxed. The storm of thoughts stopped swirling in my head and settled down into two words: cold feet. That was all it was. Cold feet.

I'VE NEVER DREAMED OF BEING A PRINCESS

I dipped into the cheese and fruit platters. My appetite was back.

My friend sat me down to do my makeup, and soon it was time for Diane to help me into my dress. It was beautiful. Not what I'd originally wanted, but Diane had insisted I try it on.

I would have been happy with a plain white dress from Macy's. "I'm not a princess," I had argued at the bridal shop. "I've never dreamed of being a princess."

"This is your wedding!" she'd scolded. Diane wanted everything perfect. She was the one who'd ordered and paid for my formal wedding invitations—after I told her I could just make them by hand.

"What is wrong with you?" she'd said then.

She repeated this at the shop, adding, "You have to wear a wedding dress!"

⌒

I tried on the simplest, "non-wedding," dresses they had, but I didn't like the way any of them looked.

"Just try this on!" Diane insisted, extending the poofy dress I had scoffed at earlier.

"Fine!" I growled, wishing this whole bridal appointment would just end.

The saleswoman helped me put it on, and as I looked in the mirror I couldn't believe how it made me feel. I walked out with a small, embarrassed smile on my face. Diane was right.

My sister and my aunt Irma came close to me, smiling.

"Oh my God, honey, you look beautiful," Irma said, beginning to cry. "Do you like it, sweetheart?"

It was a strapless gown with ruching on one side of the waist, which spread out toward the skirt in delicate waves. It was simple enough: no bling, no lace, not as poofy as I had imagined. But most of all it made me feel beautiful.

"I love it."

I spun around and watched myself waltz in the mirror. I didn't want to take it off. Irma took pictures to send to my mother in Florida. This was really happening.

⌒

This was really happening. I held on to my father's arm as we stood at the doorway waiting for the cue to go outside. It suddenly felt hard to breathe. Through the small opening in the window blinds, I could see my niece slowly walking, scattering flower petals on the aisle. I looked at my father, who was focused on looking straight ahead. He seemed nervous, too. Just outside the doorway some friends and family looked at me with bright smiles and snapped pictures. My cousin Lizzette was the only one to notice the look on my face.

"Breathe," she said, gesturing for me to take in a deep breath. We did this together, then both exhaled. I looked at her eyes as we repeated the breath: long inhale, hold, then release. The wedding march music began, and my father led me outside.

⌒

We walked around the small corner, and there he was. Gavin looked handsome in his black suit and wine-colored tie. He was smiling. I smiled back as my body and breathing relaxed.

"Who gives this woman to be married," the pastor asked as we reached the arch of white lilies.

My father responded in his thick Spanish accent, "Her mother and I."

He kissed me on the cheek and handed me over to my soon-to-be husband. My father, who had loved and treasured me all my life, who'd given me his very best, handed my heart into Gavin's care.

The music stopped. Gavin looked into my eyes as we promised each other forever love.

HE WASN'T MY TYPE

With cheers from our family and friends we walked away from the altar, our clasped hands raised in the air. Soon I was back upstairs in the little bridal room, this time with my husband. He held on to me tightly but kissed me with careful tenderness. I felt safe. "You're my husband," I said, holding his face. Neither of us discussed the morning phone call. His gentle smile was enough to make me push it out of my mind completely. This was the man I had fallen in love with.

⌣

We had met teaching gymnastics in New York City. He wasn't my type at all: I was attracted to Latin men, and Gavin was African American. After my last boyfriend, who was anti-social, I now looked for someone as silly and outgoing as I was. Gavin was an introvert, yet it was his soft, humble spirit that drew me to him as a friend. With all the loud, attention-seeking coaches in the gym, Gavin's quiet sweetness was a breath of fresh air. He played the guitar like my father, and I picked up my lessons with Gavin where my father had left off. He was my rock climbing partner, my Rollerblading buddy, and my movie companion. He taught boxing in the sports complex, and I was his loyal student. He bought me my first and last pair of boxing shoes.

I didn't have to wonder what I was doing on a Saturday night. I was hanging out with Gavin. When my first book came out, he was the first one in line to have it signed. When I sang in church, he was in the front row. I encouraged him to play guitar in public, and when he started playing the blues at open jams, I was his groupie. He was without a doubt the best friend I'd ever had. Walking with him on beautiful city nights, I would often sigh to myself, thinking, *I wish I were attracted to this man! He would make the perfect husband.* Who else would carry extra hair ties in his duffel bag just because I was always forgetting mine when I came to work? Who else would call my awkward junior-high-school pictures sweet and tell me he saw a girl always willing to smile and let her inner light shine? Who else would Rollerblade behind me, pushing my back as I stood completely still on my skates, because I was tired of blading home during the public transportation strike? As I zoomed through the city streets on my Rollerblades, with my arms spread out like a bird, he was, literally, the wind beneath my wings.

⌒⌒

During one of Gavin's boxing matches, a year into our friendship, my wish that I would find him attractive came true—a little too late. About a dozen co-workers and I were ringside watching Gavin battle it out. Everyone was cheering, but I was the loudest as I jumped up and down with each round. "Go, Gavin!" I shouted over and over again.

I recoiled with each shot he caught to his face and screamed joyously with every shot he landed. When the referee threw Gavin's hand up in victory, it was euphoric. I saw him in that boxing ring, with his pumped biceps glistening, and, for the first time, my sweet, quiet friend was a sexy beast.

Moments later, I threw my arms around him. "I'm so proud of you!" I said, squeezing him tight. Our co-workers surrounded Gavin, congratulating him—and then I heard one of them say "Where's your girlfriend?"

His response made my whole body tense up. "She missed it, but she's on her way. Got caught up in traffic."

I knew his ex-girlfriend was back in his life. They'd just recently begun to speak again, but the way he'd talked about her had made me think he wasn't very interested in getting back together with her.

"I have to go," I lied. "I have to meet a friend. But—yay, I'm so proud of you." I practically ran out of there. I did not want to see her, and the jealousy that radiated through my entire being shocked me.

KISS

L adies and gentlemen, stand to your feet for your bride and groom, Karen and Gavin!" The doors opened and the room exploded with applause as we danced in. I was overcome by the love that surrounded us.

"And now," said the DJ, "Gavin and Karen will have their first dance as husband and wife."

We held each other and smiled at our little surprise. There was a brief pause before the salsa music came on. I wiggled my shoulders and hips as Gavin stood there, pretending to be surprised. Then he took my hand like an expert salsero and twirled me around the dance floor as the room exploded in cheers and excitement again. The salsa classes we had taken regularly since we had first become friends had paid off. We laughed breathlessly after the dance and walked together to the fancy wedding table set up just for us. Our guests clinked their glasses with spoons to request a kiss from the bride and groom. We obliged.

⌒

Our first kiss had been at the train station as we were about to go in different directions. We had given each other our usual hug, except I hung on a little longer. It was a few days after his big boxing match, and my feelings had only grown stronger. As we began to let go I quietly said, "Kiss me," and he pulled me into his lips.

It was exactly a year from the time we met, and a year later we were dancing at our wedding.

BLANK CANVAS

Weeks before the wedding, my little apartment in the city underwent major changes. I emptied out a large closet and several dresser drawers to make room for my husband-to-be. I filled numerous garbage bags with old clothes, useless trinkets, broken electronics, and countless other things I no longer used. I took down from the walls framed black-and-white photos I'd shot in college, colorful canvases I'd painted in oils and acrylic, clocks and decorative mirrors. I wiped my refrigerator door clean of every magnet from California to Paris. All my traveling and adventures were now stored in a little tin can. I even changed the bedspread from a colorful print to a plain lily-white quilt. I wanted an empty canvas—free from the person I was. This would no longer be my home; it would be ours. After our vows I wanted us to rebuild together, pick the colors, hang new paintings, fill picture frames with photos of our own experiences and adventures.

My last touch in the apartment—just before I left for Diane's house—was something incredibly cliché: I sprinkled red rose petals on the bed.

Gavin carried me over the threshold our wedding night and we made love. It wasn't the first time.

BLURRING THE LINES

I was still a virgin when we started dating. At my age, that was embarrassing to admit, but that was how I was raised, and the Bible's warning against sex before marriage made sense to me. I didn't want to share that intimacy with a man who wasn't committed to me as a person, first. I'd dated and had serious relationships, but no man ever seemed worthy of breaking that promise. With each breakup I was relieved I hadn't completely crossed that line. For me, sex wasn't worth the risk of disease, pregnancy, or the feeling of being discarded after he was done with me. God had blessed my parents, who had waited for their wedding night, and they had been together for almost forty years. I wanted the same. So I made the choice to wait for my future husband, a man who would share my faith, and now I just knew I'd found him in Gavin.

He was raised in church and baptized at twelve, his mother was a Christian, and, although he hadn't gone to church in a while before we met, he went every Sunday with me. As frustrating as it was, Gavin was respectful of my decision to wait. But it wasn't easy to resist. His body was chiseled, his kisses were intoxicating, we had plenty of privacy in my apartment, and I allowed us to blur the lines of intimacy, staying clear only of intercourse. I convinced myself it was okay because he would be my future husband. I knew he'd be my partner for life with complete certainty.

∽

Gavin and I were in love. We had as much fun together as boyfriend and girlfriend as we had when we were friends—only more. We were together always and became that annoying couple who always snuggled into each other and kissed whenever we waited for the light to change at the crosswalk or sat on the same side of the booth in a diner. When we were walking together, we were holding hands. If ever I walked somewhere alone, my hand felt strange just hanging there by itself.

∽

One night as we cuddled on the couch watching a movie, Gavin said he had something he needed to tell me. He turned off the TV and I turned to his very serious face. "What is it, babe?" I asked.

"You need to know this before things go any further, because I know this is important to you." He paused and I waited for him in silence. What could this be?

"I was raised in church and stopped going for a while, as you know."

"Okay."

"When I started going with you I had to really ask myself, Do I really believe this stuff, or was I just raised to believe?"

"And?"

"And I've come to the conclusion that I just don't buy it."

I felt my insides twist. My certainty that Gavin would be my partner for life crumbled with that one sentence. How could our relationship survive if we weren't on the same page in our faith? How could he truly accept me if the most important part of my identity was nonsense to him? As sickening as it made me feel to imagine us apart, I knew we couldn't walk together if we were heading in different directions.

I didn't know what to say.

I went to the bathroom and sobbed, and Gavin quietly left.

Everything I enjoyed came to a halt. I couldn't play the guitar without crying. When other men danced with me at salsa class, I would cringe. I stopped rock climbing. I didn't have a partner to hold the rope and keep me safe anymore. Before Gavin, I was single for a few years. I'd gotten used to being alone. Now it was torture.

"Hey, it's me."

My answering machine had been blinking when I walked into the apartment. I was hoping it would be him. It was.

"Can we meet in the park to talk?"

I tried on dozens of outfits to make sure I looked good. I rarely wore makeup, but that day I carefully put on mascara, blushed my cheeks, and dabbed my lips with tinted gloss.

"Hi," I said as I walked up to him by the park entrance.

"Hi."

He kissed me on the cheek. It felt strange for my lips to be untouched.

We walked in silence to a large rock, where we sat and talked for a long time. To my surprise, he agreed that breaking up was for the best. My heart crumbled as he reaffirmed what I already knew: "We're two very different people," he said, "who want different things out of life."

We promised to stay friends and we held each other for a long time, trying to say good-bye.

But by the end of our time in the park he was kissing my lips and the tears on my cheeks. We couldn't let go. I'd made my decision, and so had he. We would find a way to make it work. But it would never be the same after that day.

YOUR FAITH WAS BENDABLE

Gavin was scheduled to go to Texas to box with the military for a few months. He would train and compete in a big boxing tournament in San Antonio. We stayed at a hotel near the base in New York the night before he left for Texas. And that's where we had sex for the first time.

"I want you to make love to me," I said quietly as we sat kissing on the edge of the bed.

Gavin straightened up and looked at me carefully. "Are you sure? I don't want you to regret it."

"I'm sure." I kissed him.

"I want to." I kissed him again.

"I'm not going to regret anything."

He laid me on the bed and took off his shirt. I took a breath and pushed out every thought that would ruin this moment. I didn't want to imagine my mother, I didn't want to think about God, or the promise of purity I'd made to him so many years ago.

I loved Gavin. And he needed to know how much I loved him. There had been a distance between us that was building. I was losing him. I could feel it. What if he went to Texas and decided not to be with me anymore? I couldn't bear it. He needed to know how much he meant to me. Before he left, I had to show him that he had me completely—my mind, my soul, and now my body.

We locked eyes as he moved over me, and in one night of defiance, pain, and ecstasy, my years of waiting were over.

⌒

Several years later, Gavin told me he had planned to break up with me while he was in Texas. He loved me but had grown tired of coming second to my beliefs. After that night in the hotel, he had changed his mind. But it wasn't just because we could now have sex.

"I stayed with you because you showed me your faith was bendable," he said. "And I could live with that."

BOXING RING

On our honeymoon, Gavin and I walked through the cobbled streets of Old San Juan, Puerto Rico. Cast-iron balconies decorated with flowers adorned each building in colors of lime, berry, orange sherbet, and lemon. We were just like the commercials for travel and leisure—Gavin in his light-blue, Caribbean guayabera shirt; me in my flowing white skirt—holding hands, without a care in the world. We lounged on powdered sand—even though Gavin wasn't a fan of the sun—ate delicious food in beautiful restaurants, and made love, guilt free. It was heaven. Simply heaven.

～

This was my second time traveling out of state with Gavin. The first time was when I'd visited him in San Antonio, Texas, where he had asked me to be his wife. We spoke a lot about marriage over the phone during those months apart, and I was glad to have some distance, since I was feeling conflicted about whether we should continue to have sex. I wanted to stay true to what I'd said that night: "I'm not going to regret anything." It was a beautiful moment for us, I'd argue whenever the guilt began to creep in. But in church, every sermon seemed to speak directly to me, and I felt torn.

As I flew out to see Gavin's big fight, I dreaded telling him that I didn't want to have sex anymore—not until we were married. I wanted to at least try, but I wasn't sure if I even had the willpower to stop, now that I was no longer a virgin.

Thankfully, he wasn't thinking about sex before his big fight. I sat with the cheering crowd as Gavin and his opponent were announced. During the first round, Gavin dominated the fight. I was cheering and screaming his name just as I had the night of his first fight.

He was confident of a win. Gavin had it all worked out in his mind: after he won, the referee would raise his hand in victory. He would call me up to the ring and he would get down on one knee. I would say yes, and the crowd would go wild, cheering loudly for us and the dramatic proposal. But that didn't happen. Gavin was knocked out cold in the third round.

～

A depressed Gavin asked me quietly to be his wife in his dreary little hotel room, and my desire to reclaim my promise to God didn't keep.

MANGOS

The last day of our honeymoon in Puerto Rico, I bought three giant mangos. They were the juiciest, most delicious mangos I'd ever had. I wanted to enjoy as many as I could before going back to the bland mangos they sold in New York City. I sat on top of the bathroom-sink counter in my bathing suit, devouring one mango after another, the juice dripping down into the drain. "Oh, my God," I shouted to Gavin, who was in the other room. "I can't believe what a craving I have for these things right now!" And then it dawned on me that I still hadn't gotten my period.

The first thing I bought when we landed in New York was a pregnancy test. It was positive. And, just like that, the honeymoon was over.

EXPECTANT MOM

"I had always wanted to be a mother."

I LIKE THE SOUND OF THREE

I had always wanted to be a mother. I was the kid who would constantly beg to hold the newborn, the teenager who loved to babysit, and the aunt who gushed over her nieces and nephews. Yet, as we stood there looking at the plus sign on the ept pregnancy test, I began to cry. They were not tears of joy.

"Hmm…That's definitely a plus sign," Gavin said, looking carefully at the stick. "Why don't you try another one?"

I grabbed the spare test from the box and ran back into the bathroom. Maybe the first one was defective. I prayed it was. Three minutes later I was in hysterics again. I fell into my husband's arms.

My husband—this was a word I was still getting used to. Now I had a new word bouncing around in my head: *mother*. Overweight mother, broke mother, tired, no-life mother nagging her husband to change the baby's diaper. What would this new word do to my life, my body, my bank account, my newborn marriage?

Gavin held me on his lap. I couldn't stop crying.

"It won't be just the two of us anymore," I said.

"I like the sound of three," Gavin said, trying to make me feel better.

⌒

I went to bed that night and put my hand on my stomach—still flat and firm. I wanted to feel the happiness I'd always imagined this moment would bring, but I just couldn't.

How could I not be overjoyed by this? I asked myself quietly in the dark of the room. I was already the worst mother in the world.

⌒

Weeks after the shock, life felt exactly the same. Other than avoiding Brie cheese, tuna fish, and chocolate, nothing really changed. I didn't even get the dreaded nausea that most mothers recall with horror. It felt dreamlike, as if the whole thing was just make-believe.

A few weeks later, the midwife poured cold goop on my still-flat stomach.

"There's your baby," she said, smiling and pointing to the small screen near the bed.

I squinted forward and examined the moving picture. I saw a little head, waving arms, and a tiny heart pulsating on the screen like a blinking light.

It didn't feel like make-believe anymore. This was actually happening inside of me. I didn't cry as perhaps I should have, seeing my unborn child for the first time, but the fog had cleared; I accepted my little unexpected and braced myself for motherhood.

NIPPLE GUARDS

I was looking at a wall of about a hundred different baby-bottle nipples: rubber, silicon, fast, slow, medium, orthodontic. I stood there frozen with the scanner in my hand and turned to my sister with bulging eyes.

"Don't ask me." Diane shrugged, looking just as lost as I felt.

We walked around the store in a daze, preparing the list for baby-shower gifts, and I asked her more questions she couldn't answer: "Will I really need that? Do I get the bouncer or swing? 'Cause I don't have room for both." And "Wow, what the heck is a nipple guard?" Soon my questions weren't about baby products anymore. *I don't think I'm ready for all of this,* I thought. *How will I know what to do? Am I going to feel as lost with a baby as I feel in this store?*

I felt overwhelmed and completely underexperienced, and I ended up leaving with just a few items scanned.

JUST MY HORMONES

Gavin sat on the couch watching a boxing match on TV. I sat down next to him but didn't snuggle into his arm as I normally did. *Why should I be the only one reaching out for a hug or a kiss?* I thought. I'd felt a bit of distance growing between us. We didn't talk as much anymore and I felt like a bother whenever I tried to spark up a conversation. At work, I passed by him and I could have sworn he gave me a look of disgust.

"Did you just give me a dirty look?" I'd asked.

But now he looked at me like I was crazy.

"What are you talking about?" he asked.

"Oh, never mind," I said, embarrassed. "It's probably my hormones."

I prayed it was my hormones, because I couldn't bear there being something wrong with our marriage now. Not while I was pregnant.

I sat on the couch for a while, waiting for him to touch me. It never came. I gave up and wrapped my arms around him, burying my head in his chest.

GOD WILL ALWAYS PROVIDE ENOUGH

I got it!" I screamed, looking at my laptop in shock. "Gavin, come here!"

"What?" he said unenthusiastically, not coming over.

"The contract! I got the book contract!"

I had submitted a children's book series through my literary agent and had been waiting for months for an answer from the publisher.

"They're offering me more than I expected!" I shrieked.

✎

As my stomach grew, I'd become concerned about working at the gym, lifting mats and spotting kids as they'd swing, leap, and flip through the air.

"You don't have to worry right now," my midwife had said at our appointment, "but the bigger you get, the more risk you'll have for back problems."

I wanted to stay as long as I could. Money was already tight with both of us working. What was going to happen when I stopped?

After church one Sunday, a group of elders stood at the altar for anyone who wanted to pray. I went directly to Mrs. Singleton, whose warm hugs always made me feel safe.

"I've never had anyone take care of me before, other than my parents," I said, "and I'm not sure he can."

I wasn't great at managing my money, but Gavin seemed to be even worse.

"What if it's not enough?"

She wrapped her hands around mine.

"You can't ever depend on yourself or your husband. God is your provider. He will open those doors for your family. Trust in him, Karen, and God will always provide enough."

I remembered her words as I looked at the screen, calculating our monthly bills. "Babe," I said in disbelief, "this is enough to keep us going well after the baby is born."

"Oh, that's really good," he said, finally coming over to look at my computer.

"So, do you want to split the bills as we've been doing, or just use the book money?"

"Let's just use the book money for now," he said.

We agreed to live off that money until it ran out, then Gavin would be responsible for the bills after that, while I took care of the baby.

I gave the gym my notice, and hoped some of the distance I'd begun to feel with Gavin would subside now that we could relax about money for a while.

BLANKET

Really, it's a boy?" I gasped during the midwife appointment.

"It sure is," she said, pointing to the screen, at what she said was a little penis. "You see that right there?"

I didn't.

Gavin and I left the appointment talking about names. We were both happy to hear it was a boy. I went to the nearest craft shop and bought rolls of light-blue yarn. I hadn't crocheted in years, but was excited to make my son a blanket. It was crooked.

As excited as I was becoming, worry had now set in. I tried not to think of the worst, but the possibilities of endless complications buzzed about my head like a persistent fly. I had no solid reason to fear. All my blood and urine tests came out normal, and I passed all my prerequisites for a normal childbirth with flying colors—I don't drink, never smoked, and I didn't live near a chemical power plant. I had, however, just turned thirty-five, the age where doctors begin to fill your head with every possible birth defect your decrepit body might produce.

I already understood that anything could happen. Just months before I found out I was pregnant, a close friend lost her baby in the third month due to fetal defects. Another dear friend who had eagerly desired to be a mother finally had her tubes tied after five miscarriages. But the fear that haunted me the most came from the young woman at my former church who delivered a stillborn. I had visited her in the hospital and she'd handed me a picture of her lifeless son wrapped in a powder-blue blanket and wearing a tiny white hat. A nurse had given her the photo along with the hat and the soft, blue blanket now cuddled in the arms of the father, who sat quietly nearby. I could never imagine the pain these women felt, and now, more than ever, I hoped I never would.

THE ONLY TIME I FEEL CLOSE TO YOU

Okay, bye," I said faintly to Gavin.

I had stopped asking him to come with me to church. It was always no. Gavin sat glued to his laptop playing another online chess opponent. The little bleeps with each move were like nails on a chalk-board to me. I'd listen to those bleeps every day, all day, as I'd clean the house by myself, watch TV alone, or lie in our bed waiting for him to lie next to me. When he did, he stayed on his side. We almost never had sex anymore. One of the few times we did, I started to cry at the end of it. "What's wrong?" he'd asked, startled, thinking he'd hurt me.

"This is the only time I feel close to you anymore," I said, wiping the tears that wouldn't stop. He rolled over with no words to comfort me.

~~

"Good-bye," I said louder, standing by the door.

A barely audible "Bye" left Gavin's mouth, but he didn't take his eyes off the screen. I walked to church by myself. My hand, which used to feel strange not holding his hand, became reaccustomed to swaying by itself.

I sat in the pew, listening to the choir sing praises to God.

"Help me, Lord," I whispered through tears. "I'm so confused." The song grew more intense and so did my sobs, until I sat leaning over, my body shaking with heartache.

~~

I didn't want to worry my family, so I mainly wrote letters to God to get the anxiety off my chest.

Dear Lord,

I have never in my life felt so uncertain about the future. I'm having a baby and my marriage is such a mystery to me. I don't know how to understand or react toward my husband.

Sometimes he seems so distant and other times so reachable. It's like a rollercoaster. There are so many issues I'm afraid to speak with him about and I'm so afraid to make things worse. Do I give him space or will that just drive us further apart? He is so closed off and will not give me a direct answer anyway, so talking to him feels pointless. I am lonely, I feel unloved and neglected. I have this child growing inside of me, and I want to know that he will be born into a loving family. But I have no security in that at all. Please give me strength for the challenges that will come my way. I'm so scared and heartbroken but I know I have to be strong if I'm going to be the mother I'm supposed to be.

Help me in each step, each day of my marriage. Guide my actions, my words. Tame my emotions even within the raging hormones of pregnancy.

Your daughter, Karen

MAMI'S LITTLE GIRL

A cascade of warm, soapy water poured down from my hair, engulfing my face. "My eyes," I whined under my breath, squeezing them tighter as my mother scrubbed my scalp. I was perched on a chair with my head in the sink, something I often did as a child. But I was no longer a little girl. Instead of washing away dirt and sweat from hours of play, my mother was washing off the brown hair dye I'd bought to get rid of scattered grays. As the water finally ran clear, she shut it off, twisted my hair like a wet rag, and draped my head with a soft towel that smelled of fabric softener. I could have easily dried my dripping hair and face alone, but my mother was on a roll. She rubbed the towel on the back of my neck, ears, mouth, and eyes, then twirled the terrycloth into a neat turban over my head. "There," she said, with a smile.

My cell phone rang. It was Gavin. "I'm home," he grunted after his long flight.

We were supposed to be on the same flight home after visiting my parents for Christmas in Florida, but I had decided to spend a few extra days with them.

Gavin and I spoke briefly, and then I went back to my mother's sweet care.

"You want some ice cream, honey?" Mami asked. "I got your favorite kind with the chocolate almonds."

"Yes!" I said getting comfy on the couch.

I'd been craving someone to pamper me and help me during my pregnancy, and my mother was more than happy to oblige. She did the little tasks for me that Gavin didn't offer to: tying my shoelaces, rubbing my back, cooking me breakfast. She had always taken care of me. I treasured these moments to be her little girl one last time, before it was my turn to take care of my own little one

LESS ALONE

I sat by the pool rubbing sunscreen on my ripe, tan belly. My little guy pushed from inside, creating a ripple of movement that looked freakishly like science fiction. He was moving more and more, and the excitement never got old.

He responded to my touch. I'd poke him. He'd poke me right back.

Gavin had not called in a few days, but with my baby moving and snuggling inside of me everywhere I went, I now felt less alone.

When I returned to New York City, I put the old paintings back on the walls, the same ones I had taken down just months ago, hoping for us to replace them with new ones. I made space in the closets once again, just like I'd done before my wedding. This time it was for tiny clothes, baby blankets, and fuzzy teddy bears. I couldn't wait to meet this new man in my life, one who was already filling my heart with more love than I'd felt from my husband.

New Mom

"His very life had begun to transform mine."

LABOR

Everything I'd read about labor and delivery promised ninety seconds of contractions maximum, with three to four minutes of relief in between. *I can handle that,* I'd thought.

The books lied. For twenty hours my body felt like a nonstop target for Taser gun practice. I was delirious with pain and in shock from the intensity of the experience. And then, after all that, they wanted me to push! As I lay there in agony—two long hours of pushing later—Diane faced my crotch with a look of pure glee on her face. "He's coming, Karen, he's coming." Gavin held my leg as the midwife instructed and everyone in the room was yelling at me to push. I then understood the cliché image of women in labor wanting to slap everyone in the room. One last bolt of sharp pain and there he was, lying bloody and gooey on my chest. Brandon had arrived.

He was screaming and I was now silent—in shock from both the torture my body had just endured and now the inconceivable reality that this little human being was actually mine.

They whisked him away before I could snap out of my daze. I stretched my neck to see Gavin near the nurse as she cleaned our son. They pressed his foot in ink for his birth certificate and pressed it once more to stamp Brandon's tiny footprint on Gavin's white T-shirt. I wanted to be over there with him, looking at our baby, but instead I lay there watching from afar as they sewed me back together.

THE LITTLE BURRITO

Hours later, after everyone left, Brandon was wrapped like a burrito and parked near my bed. Everything still felt surreal. "I don't feel like a mother yet," I had confessed to Gavin before he left, too. The baby was quiet and still, like a doll, and had been asleep for hours. I needed sleep, too, but the pain in my body was still agonizing. I'd torn quite badly when the baby came out, and I had a hemorrhoid the size of a walnut from two hours of pushing. I couldn't get comfortable, and every movement—no matter how small—was torment.

Finally I drifted off, but, just as my dream began, the little burrito woke me up. Brandon's loud, urgent cry penetrated deep inside me to a place I'd never known. It made me sit up, gritting through the pain as I inched toward my son. My pain didn't matter. Only he did. I picked him up and cradled his little body close to mine, and, to our mutual relief, the crying stopped. During that peaceful moment, as I fed my little boy, I finally felt like his mother.

ALMOND EYES

Gavin was an expert swaddler.

"All right, little man," he'd say to our irritated infant. "We're going to fold this over like this, tuck you in like that, and—Walla!"

He looked over at me with a smile, knowing I would correct his Walla with a "Voilà." I did.

Brandon, now calm and tightly wrapped, looked up at us as we sat gazing down at him. In spite of sleepless nights and the expected wailing of an infant, our son had brought serenity to our home. We were both enchanted by him—his little cries that sounded like a baby goat, his tiny arms and legs, his giant, sparkling almond-shaped eyes, his full head of spiky brown hair that curled only in the bath.

As we'd snuggle together on the couch holding our son, I could finally breathe sighs of relief and gratefulness. We were a family, and my wonderful friend Gavin had come back to me.

"Oh, look at this, look at this," Gavin said, excited, holding our fussy boy, who had begun to cry. "Someone told me to do this, and it works."

He pursed his lips and blew a gentle stream of cool air into Brandon's crying face. The crying stopped immediately as his little face looked at us in shock. The two of us laughed hysterically as Brandon continued to glare at us, then contorted his little face to cry again.

LITTLE FAMILY

I wanted to show Brandon everything. I'd stop the stroller in front of corner flower shops to take in all the colors, hold a rose near his little nose to let him smell its sweet fragrance. Art galleries, museums, and city gardens were favorites of mine as I enthusiastically introduced Brandon to the world.

Before he could even crawl, Gavin and I would take him to the playground, show him what it felt like to go down the slide, but holding him the whole way.

Gavin would plug in his electric guitar and fill our apartment with blues, then take out his acoustic and serenade our little boy with the sweetest instrumental lullabies I'd ever heard. I would dance with Brandon, sing to him, do anything I could to make him smile and hear his beautiful laugh.

Gavin went through a chef phase and cooked incredibly delicious meals. I would sit at the table looking at Brandon, who lived on breast milk, wishing I could share flavors with him along with all the sights, sounds, and smells he was being introduced to.

My first Mother's Day arrived with cards, flowers, and a romantic dinner out alone with my husband. Gavin and I were intimate again and my love for him only grew as I saw what a wonderful father he was becoming. I celebrated that in June with—among other surprises—a Father's Day card "from Brandon" expressing what an awesome daddy he was. A friend of ours came to the apartment and took amazing photographs of the three of us, and when I saw how beautiful they were it brought me to tears. All the anxiety I had before our wedding, the uncertainty and heartache I'd experienced before Brandon was born, was in the past. I didn't have to worry about those fears of not being a family. We were.

"Thank you, Lord," I'd pray in humble gratitude. "Thank you for my little family."

MAMI AND PAPI

B randon cried and squirmed in my arms most of the flight. I was tired, frustrated, and weighed down with bags. But all of that lifted the moment I saw Mami and Papi waiting with giant smiles at the gate.

They covered me in hugs and kisses mixed with laughter. Mami took Brandon out of the stroller and danced with him, singing "You Are My Sunshine." The difficulty he'd given me on the plane had disappeared and he beamed at my mother with his sparkling, almond eyes, drool streaming from his giggling lips.

⌒

Before I was married, I had lived with my parents longer than I care to admit. My mom and I bumped heads quite a bit, and when I finally lived on my own it was a welcome separation. Our relationship finally became what I thought it should be at my age: phone calls and weekly visits when they still lived in New York. When they moved to Florida, my independence was still too fresh for their distance to affect me.

⌒

Weeks before my flight, Gavin had become distant again. There were days when I'd build up the courage to talk to him, but just before I'd open my mouth, he was sweet and funny again. I'd silently scold myself for reading into his silences and creating problems that weren't there, but then it would happen all over again. I didn't trust my emotions. Maybe I was just tired from months of sleepless nights, stumbling to the crib in a haze to feed the baby night after night.

I watched what I said, and what I did around him. I tried to give enough affection to let him know I still loved him, but not too much, so I wouldn't suffocate him. I asked him to help me with Brandon only if it was absolutely necessary. I didn't want him to feel overwhelmed by his parental responsibilities.

⌒

Papi took my bag and kissed me gently on the cheek. *"Hola, mi amor,"* he said, then walked with me arm-in-arm to the car. I wondered if my mother went through this with Papi when I was born.

We drove past rows of palm trees and I settled in the back as cozy as Brandon was, comfy and dozing off in his car seat.

"Go straight, Geño!" my mom yelled as my father was about to make a right.

"*Pero,* Connie, it's this way!" he protested.

"No it's not, Gene. You make a right at the next light, not this one."

I giggled as I watched them bicker about directions. It was an expected routine in the car, but there was never a heaviness in their arguing—not even when I was growing up.

"Honey, did you call Gavin to let him know you arrived safely?" my mother asked.

I had never told her or my father about my issues with Gavin. I didn't want them to worry or feel sorry for me. "I don't think he cares if I call," I felt like saying. But I just smiled and promised to call him when I got to the house.

⌒

Brandon slapped the water in the pool with his little wild hands, then shook his head, squinting his eyes as if someone else had splashed his face.

My mother took videos and pictures of my sweet boy everywhere we went—the beach, the aquarium, Walmart. It didn't matter where we were; there was always a wonderful moment we wanted to capture with this little baby who had filled our hearts with so much joy.

I took pictures of my parents with him. I enjoyed watching them with Brandon as they danced with him, sang to him, and rocked him to sleep. The tenderness they had brought to my own childhood came back strong those few weeks in Florida, and I was grateful my son could experience that as well.

⌒

The excitement we had at the airport just weeks before now turned somber.

"Bye, Mami. Thank you for everything," I said, trying not to cry.

"Not good-bye," she said, her voice cracking with emotion. "See you later."

We held each other tight, tears falling on each other's shoulders.

Papi hugged me, too, then tucked money into my hand.

"No, Papi," I argued. "I'm fine! I don't need this!" I did.

He refused to take it back.

They took turns holding Brandon, giving him one last embrace.

I looked out the window as the airplane rolled away from the airport. My body pushed back into my seat as the plane sped forward at full velocity, racing away from the comfort and security of my parents.

I ached for Brandon, who would feel their love only in short visits; I ached for them, because I knew how much they would miss Brandon. But mostly I was heartbroken for myself.

I felt like a little girl who was lost without them. A separation I once welcomed years ago was now unbearable. I could never have imagined that so many years after gaining my independence I would so desperately want and need my mom and dad.

YOU'RE SO IGNORANT

She's so tiny!" I squealed, looking at my newborn niece. My sister-in-law Alina had given birth to a beautiful baby girl, and my six-month-old—who'd felt tiny just moments before—now seemed gigantic next to her.

"Come here, Bran Bran," my mother-in-law, Evelyn, said, reaching out to hold her grandson. My arms were now free, and I carefully scooped up the newborn to my chest. She curled into a little ball, just like Brandon used to do, and I wondered how he'd grown so fast. Gavin's whole family was there, but he was not. After absorbing all that newborn sweetness, I gave my niece a kiss on the head and handed her back to my sister-in-law. Evelyn was still playing with Brandon, so I went out into the hallway to call Gavin.

"Hi," I said when he picked up. "Everybody's here. Are you coming?"

"No," he replied, and gave an excuse I couldn't understand.

"She's your sister," I said.

"I know she's my sister."

I left it alone and hung up the phone.

Weeks later, Gavin and I went to his mother's house. The baby was there. It was the first time he'd seen her, but he didn't pick her up.

That night I couldn't hold it in. It broke my heart. "I don't under-stand why it took so long for you to see your own niece. I was there the day she was born! And then when you finally see her, you don't even pick her up? What is that?"

Gavin, who had never raised his voice, answered me with more bite than I was expecting. "You're so ignorant," he spat. "Not everybody shows love the same way you do."

I was silenced. I didn't know how to respond. But as bitter the taste of his message to me was, I completely got it. I tried to accept it and even find a bit of hope in it. Gavin did not love like me. Not even a little bit. Not like anyone I'd ever known. But perhaps deep down he did have love for his family—for me—and I just hadn't learned yet how to interpret his way of showing it.

THE DAY MY IN-LAWS BECAME MY FAMILY

Brandon was eight months old, and I still hadn't lost the weight from my pregnancy. "It's a good thing you're a personal trainer," I had joked with Gavin after I gave birth. But the workouts never happened.

I hated the flab on my belly and felt insecure when I made love to Gavin. His tight, muscular body was too much of a contrast to my soft, squishy folds.

But it was Thanksgiving, and not the time to start thinking of diets.

As much as I wanted to spend the holidays with my family this year, Gavin's oldest sister was visiting New York, and our apartment was bigger than my mother-in-law's. I reluctantly agreed to host.

My first Thanksgiving with my in-laws—the year before—had depressed me. I'd wanted to be with my family, and I craved the Latin dishes that were missing from the table. I had been in my second trimester of pregnancy with Brandon and perhaps my hormones were raging, but it didn't feel like Thanksgiving, and, as wonderful as his family was to me, all I wanted to do was be with mine.

I vowed not to have another sad Thanksgiving like the year before, even if I wasn't with my family again. That morning my mother-in-law, Evelyn, and my sisters-in-law, Alina, Kira, and Liza, arrived early, and we began to cook. They prepared the turkey and the other traditional dishes, while I made a variety of Latin dishes to go with them.

We danced around one another in the kitchen, talking and laughing as we chopped, mixed, and fussed over the stove. The bustle and commotion were very familiar to me, and I was enjoying myself.

The more people arrived, the more fun we had. The wonderful chaos felt familiar, just like my own family. I organized group games and everyone enthusiastically participated. We enjoyed the delicious food, and my Latin dishes were a hit! Everyone took turns holding Brandon, and he giggled in delight all day as they made silly faces and tossed him in the air. The family was in awe as Gavin put Brandon on the floor and they watched him take two or three wobbly steps toward me.

"I'm not surprised," Evelyn said with a proud smile. "Gavin walked at eight months, too! He's just like his daddy!".

The day was a far cry from the sad, emotional holiday I'd endured the year before. That Thanksgiving, I had a lot to be thankful for. It was the day my in-laws became my family.

"I had so much fun with you guys," I said to Liza as we were cleaning up. "Last year I was a hormonal wreck! Thank God I wasn't pregnant this time!"

Both of us laughed—neither one of us knew I was pregnant again.

POSITIVE

Ms. Singleton met me at the church. My body felt strangely familiar, and I had asked her to meet me there to confirm my fears.

"Hi, sweetheart," she said, hugging me as I walked into the Sunday school room. I held on to her hug for a long time. I was afraid to let go and take the test.

I'd confided in her all the ups and downs of my marriage, all the struggles and stresses of motherhood, and now the possibility that I may be pregnant again.

I took out the pregnancy test from the bag; my hands were shaking.

"Go ahead, honey," she said softly. "I'll be right here."

Two minutes later I walked over to her and we looked at the stick together, waiting to see what it said about my future: another baby, more stress I couldn't handle, the final wound to my dying marriage?

Positive.

"Congratulations!" she shouted, hoping I would share in her joy.

I crumbled into her arms and sobbed.

⌒

I already had my hands full with Brandon and barely had time for a shower, let alone another child. As my stomach grew, so did my bitterness. I wasn't fascinated or curious about pregnancy, as I had been before. I already knew "What to Expect When You're Expecting" and I hated every bit of it. I didn't want to eat green vegetables or hear people say "You shouldn't eat that candy bar; it's not good for the baby." I didn't want to wear frumpy maternity clothes, feel tired, sleep uncomfortably, or waddle like a penguin.

Gavin took the news as I expected. He wasn't visibly happy or upset. He just shrugged and accepted it with his usual poker face. But I already knew that, along with my growing belly, his quiet resentment for me would grow as well.

UPSTATE

Brandon looked through the window hypnotized, watching the buildings give way to mountains and trees. In a little over an hour I would be with Diane, my aunt Irma, her son Kevin, who was more of a brother than a cousin, and his three children I called my niece and nephews.

My ache for family had grown in the quiet of my apartment. I grew up with the sweet chaos of family around me all the time, and had always envisioned my own child enjoying the same. But with my parents in Florida and the rest of the family Upstate, that wasn't the reality.

⌒

I pushed the stroller out of the train when we arrived, looking past the line of cars for the blue minivan. "Brandon!" my niece and nephews screamed. They used to scream "Titi Karen!" when I arrived, but I was happy to pass that over to my baby boy.

Diane came over and gave me a bear hug; Kevin grabbed the bags and put them in the trunk.

I took in a deep breath, happy for the change in the air. It wasn't just the country sky. I felt at ease. I could talk freely and not be ignored or wonder if I was bothering anyone with my silly conversation. I could wear what I wanted without feeling insecure or unattractive. With them I could be completely myself; I could relax and finally breathe.

Irma stepped out of the car with a small wince. She'd been struggling with some medical issues, but it didn't stop the look of pure joy on her face at seeing me.

"You hungry?" Kevin asked as we all settled in the car.

"Yes," I said, smiling at the excitement of the kids in the back with Brandon. "I'm starving."

There, surrounded by mountains, trees, and my beautiful family, I didn't have to try to be loved. I just was.

I'M YOUR HUSBAND

I sat with Brandon in the corner of the gym, watching Gavin train in the boxing ring. We were going to a friend's house afterwards to watch a big boxing match on HBO, and we'd decided to meet at the gym first.

"Look at Daddy," I said to Brandon, who sat fussing on my lap.

I felt out of place as I sat there with my baby and my pregnancy fat protruding from my belly and hips. Everyone was fit and full of energy, while I looked as tired as I felt.

I felt such pride as I watched my husband in the ring, as much pride as I felt that first time I saw him fight—the night my heart began to flutter for him. My heart felt the same flutter, but was weighed down with the growing feeling that his heart no longer fluttered for me.

Gavin ducked through the ropes and walked toward us, sweaty and slightly breathless.

He pecked me on the lips, then took Brandon in his arms.

"Hey, look at the little man!" cried one of the boxers.

Gavin smiled and moved one of Brandon's arms so that it looked like he was boxing. More people gathered around. I stood smiling behind them.

One of the female instructors named Cali made goo-goo sounds at Brandon and waved to me. As she spoke to Gavin, it was obvious she was upset by one of their co-workers. He listened carefully, with the same sympathetic expression I used to know. He made a joke to lighten her mood and make her feel better. She tapped him on the arm, smiling.

"Not funny," she scolded.

I watched them—two friends at the gym, just like we used to be. His gestures, his smile, his carefree body language made my soul ache. I missed my friend Gavin. I missed how special my friend made me feel. I envied this new friend, who got to have this wonderful part of him, while I went home with the heavy, quiet, dark cloud of the man he'd become around me. I felt like his burden, and the very thought made me shrink inside.

"I think I'm a little jealous," I chuckled as we walked to the train station, awkwardly unsure about how to express what I felt.

He pursed his lips and rolled his eyes. He was not amused.

"Not jealous like that," I tried to clarify. "I wish we could be friends like that again."

"Well, I'm not your friend," he said, pushing the stroller. Then he looked at me, the smile for Cali now transformed into the usual look of annoyance reserved for me. "I'm your husband."

That night I wrote him a letter.

⌒

Gavin,

My comments about Cali have less to do with jealously and more to do with the way I feel in our relationship. I don't feel secure in our marriage and it's not hard to see why.

You were thinking about not showing up to our wedding that same day. Our sex life is practically non-existent. You've rejected me sexually—making me feel undesirable and sexually insecure. The only time you hold me is at night for a few minutes—sometimes seconds before you go to sleep. I feel starved for your affection and attention. You never compliment me, always criticize me, and make me feel like I'm an idiot. You don't try to alleviate my pregnancy aches, making me feel like you don't care if I'm in pain. You don't talk about your feelings with me, and most things I do seem to annoy you. I feel like you don't want to be with me and I'm extremely insecure about our future.

I miss our friendship more than anything, and to see you with Cali tonight laughing and communicating in a way that WE used to, was hard to watch.

I didn't finish the letter. He would dismiss it, I knew. I was whining and being ridiculous. I folded the paper neatly, put it in my dresser drawer. Soon there would be a collection of letters filled with passion, pleading, anger, and frustration, each one meant for him to read. But I never gave him a single one.

BRANDON'S FIRST BIRTHDAY

Brandon would cry anytime we sang "Happy Birthday." He would look around with his big eyes getting bigger, his lower lip would pop out, and then he'd just wail. He did not disappoint on his big day. We lit the Elmo cake, and over two dozen friends and family sang to Brandon. Like clockwork: the eyes, the lip, the tears. We all laughed and clapped. Gavin and I blew out the candles.

My baby was a one-year-old.

"Why are you making such a big party?" Gavin had asked as I busied myself with the planning and preparations. "He won't even remember his first birthday."

But this party was as much for me as it was for him. This was my first anniversary as a mom, and this little boy covered in sweet buttercream was the one who'd made me a mother. I fought the lump in my throat all day. My son was my constant companion, my best friend. His very life had begun to transform mine. When my heart was breaking, he was able to mend it with his sweet laughter. When he needed me, I understood my worth; with each milestone I understood the true meaning of pride. When I was too tired or overwhelmed, my love for him kept me going. I was able to do more than I ever thought possible because I knew it was what my son deserved. As I watched him grow I knew I was growing as a mother, too.

I shadowed Brandon as he walked around the gym. We both climbed into the large pool filled with colorful balls. Diane came over with the camera.

"Say cheese!" she cried. I squeezed him in close to me. There was no one else closer.

MUSIC PLAYGROUP

I browsed through the store of adorable shirts with trains and dinosaurs printed on the front. I placed a hat on Brandon and he looked like a miniature paperboy from the 1930s. I never spent a lot of money on myself (even before I became a mom), but the allure of spending for Brandon was a whole other story.

The money from my book deal had run out, and we now had to depend on Gavin for all our financial needs. His income was only enough for the essentials, and the fun I used to have shopping for my son came to a sudden halt.

There was no extra money for new toys or books.

"He doesn't need any more," Gavin reminded me. But that didn't make it any easier. Money for our daily excursions took a hit, too. Parks are free, but paying entrance fees for children's museums, mommy-and-me classes, and anything else fun that would cost money was out.

I'd meet up with other moms as we'd follow our little ones around monkey bars, up ladders, and down slides. Afterwards they'd go out for lunch.

"I can't today," I'd say, pushing the stroller home to make peanut-butter-and-jelly sandwiches for both of us.

I felt helpless, and frustrated. I didn't want to resent Gavin over our finances; we already had enough issues in our relationship. Something had to be done.

"Help me figure this out, Lord," I prayed.

I thought about the gifts God had given me. Surely I could use those talents to help our situation.

I pulled out my guitar. Brandon loved it when I sang to him. Maybe other kids would, too.

⌒⌒

I advertised my first trial music class through a moms' meet-up group on-line. I pushed the stroller to the park with my guitar strapped to my back and my six-month belly protruding out in front. I laid out a blanket and spread percussion noisemakers on top. Brandon went right for them, shaking them and massaging them into his teething gums.

I sat down by myself and picked at my guitar, doubting anyone would show up. Then, suddenly—like a parade—a group of strollers and moms made their way to the fenced-in lawn between two large oak trees.

I sang, read stories, and blew bubbles. Week after week, they paid to come back.

In addition to my music playgroup, I painted and sold onesies—the designs I'd created for Brandon's clothes. I painted tiny faces at birthday parties and created a handful of other projects to make extra money.

A tight budget was the price I had to pay to be a stay-at-home mom. But even though I didn't get paid to be a mother, I was grateful that God made a way for me to stay with my son and do my job well.

WHEN IT WAS JUST THE TWO OF US

It was almost time to give birth, and I began to grieve the relationship I had with Brandon. It would never be the same again. I couldn't give him all of my attention. This faceless baby I didn't know yet would be taking me away from my little boy.

"Brandon—wait, honey!" I cried as he sped away like a little Olympic runner.

Trying to keep up with my speedy one-year-old was becoming more of a challenge. Picking him up was becoming near impossible. This baby wasn't even born yet and he was already getting in the way.

I sat down and wrote in Brandon's baby book as he napped nearby. My hormones were in full effect. I wiped away tears as I wrote him what felt like a good-bye letter. "I had so much fun watching you grow this past year and a half," I wrote. I told him about all the adventures we had—just the two of us. I wrote how amazed I was by him, how he made me laugh when he danced around and finished his routine on the floor with one leg up as his grand finale. "I will always remember and treasure this time, when it was the two of us. I love you, baby. Mama."

ALOHA

My belly felt ready to burst: skin stretched like a drum, round and enormous.

Just days before my due date, my parents arrived to welcome their second grandson. Our one-bedroom apartment was cramped with new baby gear, suitcases, and us!

I was excited to have my mother and father here, but visits with anyone in my home always felt slightly awkward. Gavin wasn't a fan of hosting, which made it uncomfortable, especially with my parents.

⌒

Years before I was married, a group from Hawaii had come to my church and greeted us at the doors with beautiful shell leis. They put them over our heads with a heartfelt "Aloha," and it made me feel so special. I hung the shell lei on my door as a reminder to make everyone who walked into my home feel special and loved. But with Gavin's indifference and lack of conversation, I felt like I needed to work overtime for them to feel at home.

THINGS BETWEEN US

H e doesn't really do much, does he?" my mother complained, looking over at Gavin playing chess on his computer while my father washed the dishes.

"What are you going to do when we leave?"

I hated that they had to witness the tension in our marriage. And with my parents there, the tension and my resentment grew.

"Can't you talk to them just a little bit?" I'd plead with Gavin. "You're making them feel like they're not wanted here."

"Are you kidding me?" I'd hiss when he complained about my father always looking for something to fix and clean. "At least he's trying to be helpful!"

I wished my parents would leave so I wouldn't be caught in the middle, yet I wanted them there, and I needed their help.

My bitterness toward Gavin reached a point where I knew something needed to be done. I couldn't watch us spiral downward, not with another child on the way. I needed to let him know what I was feeling. I wrote a letter, but this time, instead of stuffing it in a drawer, I asked him to take a walk with me while my parents took care of Brandon. We walked for a bit and then I said, "I want to read something to you."

Sitting on a bench, I unfolded the letter and started to read.

Dear Gavin,

There are a few things I wanted to say to you, and, as you know, I express myself better and more clearly by writing instead of speech that usually gets jumbled and scattered. I am of course very aware that we don't have the most stable relationship. I'm not always confident in your love for me, and sometimes question my feelings for you. There are times I don't see a future for us, and at times—in my disappointment in our relationship—wish that moment would come where we just lived separate lives. But then there are times that remind me how much you mean to me, and how badly I desire for us to stay together and be a family. Some of these moments are when you make me laugh, when I feel the emotion in your soul through your beautiful music, when I see your passion for learning new things, when we're intimate, and the times when you're not feeling well, because my instinct is to make you feel better. These are the times I realize that, while I don't always feel it, my love for you is very much there. Even if the future doesn't see us through, I will always love you for the friendship we once had, and the father you've become.

I say this now, because I have a feeling things between us will get worse after the baby is born. I want you to know how I feel before this potential storm begins, and my desire to get through it, and enjoy happier times in the future. I hope we'll take care of each other, be patient and kind with each other, have fun together like we used to, and grow as a couple and as individuals. This is my hope and prayer, but more than anything, my deepest desire is that, despite any frustration or disappointment I've caused in your life, you have the same hopes, too.

Gavin looked at me with a small smile. "Come here. You worry too much," he said with a chuckle and a hug that I hoped meant he did.

MOTHER OF TWO

"What is this sleep you speak of?"

WE HAVE TO GO NOW

I woke up and I knew. I'm having this baby today. It was four in the morning and I didn't wake anyone up. I quietly got out of bed, then tiptoed past my parents. Giving birth to Brandon took forever, so I didn't want anyone to lose sleep over a contraction. I took a long bath and got dressed.

"Are you okay?" my mother whispered as I poured myself a glass of water in the kitchen.

"I'm in labor," I said.

"What?" she shrieked.

Little by little everyone got up and I convinced them I was okay. I didn't want to go to the hospital yet.

A few phone calls and a Facebook post later, things had drastically changed.

"Okay, we have to go now," I said, trying not to freak anyone out but with enough urgency to let them know I was serious.

Gavin hailed a cab and we all piled in. I felt a need to push and started to panic. "Oh my God, oh my God! I'm going to give birth in the cab!"

"Please hurry!" my mother pleaded with the driver. It was like a scene right out of a Lifetime melodrama.

Gavin ran for a wheelchair as I wobbled toward the hospital door, and just fifteen minutes later Tyler was in my arms.

TYLER

Joyless. I had been completely joyless as I'd waited for Tyler to be born.

The irony is almost too much, because from the moment I held my son, he filled me up with so much joy it made my heart just want to explode.

I knew I would endure every pain, emotion, tension, or discomfort and even double it for the honor of holding my sweet boy. He was absolutely beautiful and perfect in every way.

"Mami!" Brandon came running into the room followed by my mother.

He climbed onto the bed and I panicked for a moment.

"Mami, wash his hands," I begged.

"We just did," she assured me.

The little boy I had been writing a sentimental good-bye letter to just days before now seemed like a large ogre I needed to protect Tyler from.

"Gentle," I warned as he reached out his hands to touch his brother.

He was.

"Bebe," he said, smiling up at me. His excitement and gentleness let me relax. I held them both in my arms for the first time in that hospital bed. My boys.

"Ban-don kiss bebe," Brandon said, leaning over to Tyler. And with a sweet kiss on his brother's forehead, he sealed a bond of brotherhood that would only grow stronger with each day.

LOVE IN CHINESE

The mom who shared my room spoke no English. But I didn't need to understand Chinese to understand the excitement she shared with her husband over their newborn. Her husband brought her food from outside, made silly noises as he held his daughter, squeezed next to his wife in the narrow bed, and stayed way beyond visiting hours. They had to tell him to leave.

My parents had left with Brandon a few hours after I gave birth. My mother wanted to stay, but my father wouldn't know what to do with my eighteen-month-old all by himself. Gavin stayed for a bit, but then went to work. Afterwards he worked out, and didn't come back until the next day for another brief visit. I stayed in the hospital for two days, mostly alone, forced to listen to love in Chinese.

CIRCUMCISION

As I waited for the doctor to take Tyler away for his circumcision, I felt like Isaac preparing to sacrifice Jacob. I held my newborn close to my body, tears baptizing his head. I didn't have to put him through this pain. The doctor had made it clear there were no health benefits and it was strictly for cosmetic, cultural, or religious reasons. So why was I doing this? Gavin was clear on his reasoning—the locker room and the girl—but what was mine? *Circumcision is so Old Testament,* I argued with myself. *It's not even relevant today.*

Before I could finish the debate in my head, it was time. The doctor came in with a sweet smile on her pretty face, but she might as well have been wearing a black hooded mask and carrying a hacksaw.

"He'll be right back," she said. And with that she rolled Tyler away, leaving me in postpartum hysterics.

⌒

That was the second circumcision I had to torture myself over. But before the wound even healed, we were back in the hospital again. Tyler was jaundiced and had to go under the lights. He lay there bare, with only a diaper, his eyes covered with a tiny blindfold. My little baby would flail his legs and reach out his tiny arms, screeching to be held. But I couldn't pick him up. They'd poked his tiny foot over and over to test the levels in his blood, and I would wince with each prick. I didn't want to see him in the hospital anymore. He needed to be home in his own crib. I didn't know what to expect at home, now that we were a family of four. Gavin didn't have the same enthusiasm he'd had when Brandon was born, and part of me already expected that. But none of that mattered now. I was tired of fixating on how Gavin felt about everything. I didn't care anymore how he responded to me. I couldn't control how he felt or what would unfold in our marriage. As I sat there now watching my tiny son surrounded by doctors, all I wanted was to be home with my two boys and be their mom.

MY TIME WITH TYLER

S leep?" I asked Diane when she asked me what bedroom I wanted to sleep in with Gavin and the boys. "What is this sleep you speak of?"

We'd taken the Metro North train Upstate for Thanksgiving, and Diane led me to the bigger guest room in her house. I looked at the bed and wanted to collapse right there, but Tyler was screaming to be fed. Gavin put the bags down, then took Brandon downstairs. I could hear my niece and nephews take over as he ran and burst into laughter.

I closed the door and laid Tyler down on the comforter as he continued to howl. Once I was comfortable with pillows on my back and lap, I cradled him to my body and began to breast-feed. I leaned back and took a long breath. As the milk flowed from my body, so did my stress from our commute with two crying children, a double stroller, and numerous bags.

I absolutely loved this time with my baby. It was a relief to my body and mind, but most of all this was my time with Tyler—just him and me. When I fed him I could hold him close, caress his soft hair, and just gaze at his beautiful little face.

Time alone with him was rare at home, even when I fed him. While Tyler was my Zen baby, content alone in his bouncer simply to people-watch, Brandon demanded all of my attention all the time.

Feedings were interrupted almost like clockwork. The moment Tyler would began to nurse, Brandon would find a way to interrupt: thrusting his arm elbow-deep into a jar of peanut butter left open on the table, climbing on my back, or screaming for me to get up and follow him somewhere.

"You know," I'd complain to him as if he understood, "no one ever interrupted you when you were breast-feeding!"

⌒

Tyler looked up at me, smiling with his eyes half closed. He nursed a bit more, enjoying this peaceful time as much as I was, then fell asleep in my arms. With the scent of Thanksgiving slowly rising and my family giving Brandon all the attention he desired, I snuggled into my baby's little body and fell asleep.

THE MISSING DISH

As I looked at the Thanksgiving table filled with traditional holiday food and delicious Latin dishes as well, I felt thankful—thankful I was Puerto Rican! I couldn't wait to fill my plate with pasteles, pernil, and arroz con gandules. How I'd missed Thanksgiving with my family and the amazing cooks who were now laughing and chatting around the table. The only dish missing was my aunt Irma's staple Thanksgiving recipe: sweet-potato-and-walnut purée in a pie dish topped with toasted marshmallows. My incredible aunt, who was more like a second mother to me, passed away just before Tyler was born. I missed her presence with the family, her funny stories, her contagious laugh, and her feisty spirit. Life wasn't the same without her.

Irma was the one who made me ride my first roller coaster. I was crying in line, but she insisted I would love it. She was right. Irma took me to my first Broadway musical and taught me to walk in heels and sway my hips. I'm not sure I ever mastered it. I never packed pajamas to sleep over at her house. I felt too cozy in hers. She booked the vacations, took us to festivals—childhood would have been boring without her. I called her by her name—Irma, never Auntie or Titi—but she was nothing less than a mother to me.

She'd been sick for half of her life, but she never let it stop her from living to the fullest. I remember seeing her in pain at a county fair, and I begged for us to leave so she could rest. "Are you kidding me?" she barked. "If I went home every time I felt pain, I'd never go anywhere." She was teaching me resilience before I ever had to use it.

My uncle Edwin quieted everyone down to bless the food, but just before he did, Diane added the last dish to the table.

"You made it!" I screamed, looking at the pie dish with toasted marshmallows on top.

"I had to," Diane said. "It's not Thanksgiving without it."

Edwin prayed for the food and the family. I said an extra prayer in my heart, thanking him for the years I had been blessed to have Irma in my life.

RSV

Tyler looked at me with panic in his eyes. He was crying, but softly, because he didn't have the breath to express the level of distress he was in. He wasn't gasping for air, or turning blue, but as I looked at him I found myself breathing extra hard, as if helping him along. Gavin was working, so I called my neighbor to come down.

"I don't know what's going on," I said, packing a small bag in a frenzy. "I can't tell if he's really having trouble breathing, or if I'm just imagining things, but something doesn't feel right." She looked at Tyler and couldn't tell, either.

"Honey, if you think something is wrong then it probably is," she insisted. "Never question your instincts as a mother."

I ran out the door and grabbed a cab. It was late, and I felt bad for bothering my neighbor. Was I just a neurotic mother?

I wasn't. Tyler's oxygen levels were extremely low, and, at his delicate age, it was serious. We were admitted and placed in isolation, and Tyler was hooked up to an oxygen tank. He had RSV (respiratory syncytial virus).

⌒

They discharged him after two days in the hospital, but I felt uneasy.

"His stomach is still pushing out when he breathes," I said, pointing out one of the signs they'd shown me to recognize distress.

"Yes," the doctor said. "He's going to do that. He still has the virus. But his levels are much better."

"But then how will I know to come back?"

They couldn't give me a clear answer.

I reluctantly bundled up my baby and took him home, but just five hours later I called my neighbor back downstairs.

"They just discharged him," I told her as I guided Tyler's tiny arms through the sleeves of his snowsuit again. "They're going to think I'm crazy."

"Who cares?" she said softly, rubbing my back. "You are his mother. Trust yourself. You know what's best for your son."

In minutes we were back in the emergency room. Tyler's oxygen levels were lower than ever before, and they admitted him once again.

I cradled my baby, who was sleeping peacefully, oxygen tubes in his little nose. I broke down.

There were so many emotions pouring out of me. I was scared for Tyler. He was still so new—only two months old. I was angry with the doctors for discharging him early, angry with myself for letting them, even when I felt uneasy about leaving. I felt foolish for questioning myself, but proud and relieved that, despite my doubts, I had taken action anyway.

The words of my neighbor and friend echoed in my ear: "You are his mother. Trust yourself. You know what's best for your son." In that moment I owned those words. God put this little life in my care and placed a gift of intuition in my heart's core. I promised myself, and my little boy, that I would trust in that gift like never before.

BRANDON

Gavin and I took the boys to the gym to let Brandon jump around. We'd been cooped up because of snow for a few days, and we needed to let him burn off his incredible energy. With Tyler strapped to me, I watched Gavin play with Brandon.

"Oh, he's so cute!" my old co-worker exclaimed, coming over to me to look at the baby, who was asleep.

"Thank you," I said, adjusting Tyler's head to make him more comfortable.

"And Brandon!" she continued. "He's amazing!"

I smiled and agreed. He really was.

My little boy, who was almost two years old, wowed anyone who saw him. He could dribble a basketball like a pro, flip forward into the foam pit after jumping high on the trampoline, and do a pull-over on the bar with just a light spot. He could hit a Wiffle ball clear across the room with his red baseball bat, and would stick landings on both feet after jumping off chairs, beds, and other things that seemed too high to land from without a fall.

Gavin took Tyler, who had woken up, so I could play with Brandon, too. He and I had hit a good patch, and I treasured those moments as a happy family because I never knew when times would change.

The four of us sat on the trampoline, pushing our bodies gently up and down for Tyler. He lit up, and so did Brandon. "Ty-yer jumpin'" he said, then he ran off and jumped into the foam pit for us to chase him.

BATH TIME

> "Only the most ancient love on earth
> will wash and comb the statue of the children."
> —Pablo Neruda, "To Wash a Child"

Come on, Brandon," I said after filling the tub with water and bubbles. "It's bath time." Brandon ran, squealing, toward the bathroom.

I could never seem to pull off his shirt and diaper fast enough as he waited to get into the tub. Tyler would get excited, too, reaching down from my arms or crawling toward the tub, trying to get in himself.

Between spit-up in the folds of Tyler's chubby neck, food in Brandon's hair, and offensive diaper changes from them both, a sweet-smelling baby did not happen on its own.

I placed Tyler in with Brandon, and the splashing began immediately, with giggles and belly laughs. The bathtub is where Brandon made his little brother laugh for the first time.

I sat down on the tiles as I let them play in the bubbly water filled with cups and squeaky toys. I allowed their splashing to spray my face and lap. I didn't mind. That was my time to breathe—Tyler wasn't crawling around finding interesting things to put in his mouth, and Brandon wasn't climbing on the furniture. In the tub they were happy, they were together, and, best of all, they were contained!

One by one I lathered them up, obviously annoying them, interfering with their fun. I washed their faces, massaged soap into their hair, their bellies, their legs; and little by little they became new again. Gavin came in to scoop up Tyler, and I put Brandon on the soft towel I'd draped over my shoulder. I wrapped him up and kissed his little wet face.

"Who's the cutest and cleanest little boy in the world?" I said, squeezing him as we looked in the mirror.

"Ban-don!" he shouted.

I breathed in the sweet fragrance of my son, then joined Gavin and Tyler in the bedroom.

With both naked boys on the bed, we sprinkled their bodies with baby powder and put on freshly washed pairs of pajamas.

No one was allowed on the floor after bath time. I couldn't ruin the perfection of it all with dusty feet. There would be time enough the next day for mud, sand, and sticky food—it was a never-ending battle between dirt and bubbles.

FLORIDA

Gavin made a tent with bedsheets draped over the kitchen chairs for the boys.

He crawled through, and Brandon and Tyler followed him in fits of laughter. I smiled over at the scene, then refocused on the enormous task at hand: packing.

The idea of traveling—before the boys—used to relax me. Now it stressed me out before the bags were even packed. I checked my list, which had grown day by day, and crossed out each item as it went in the bag.

"How am I going to fit all this crap in here?" I mumbled. I could never believe how much I had to squeeze into the luggage, and of course almost none of it was for me. I'd end up wearing the same jeans for days just so I had enough room to bring the breast pump.

The next day Gavin's mother drove us to the airport.

"Don't cry, Ty Ty," she shouted in baby talk as Tyler wailed in his car seat.

He hated being in the car, and with each car ride we'd sing a never-ending cabaret of "Itsy Bitsy Spider" and "The Wheels on the Bus" just to keep him from screaming.

Evelyn pulled over at the drop-off area and quickly went to console Tyler while Gavin and I got the bags.

"Are you going to be able to do this by yourself?" she asked, putting Tyler in his stroller. He was still crying.

"Yeah, I'll be okay," I said.

I gave her a hug and kissed Gavin good-bye.

"Say see you later to Daddy," I told Brandon as Evelyn strapped him into the rolling car seat.

"See yay-tah," Brandon said.

With one hand I pushed Tyler's stroller, its handles draped with a heavy carry-on, the other hand pulled Brandon in the rolling car seat, and on my shoulders sat a giant oversized backpack that looked like a boulder.

"Here we go," I said as I walked through the airport. The burdensome sight of the three of us turned heads until I checked in the bag and the stroller and got on the plane.

My parents had bought us tickets to see them in Florida. I couldn't wait to escape the cold and let Brandon run free on a warm playground. My cabin fever with the boys that winter was reaching levels of insanity.

My parents greeted us at the airport with the usual celebration, bickered in the car about directions yet again, and had a hot Puerto Rican meal waiting for us when we got to their house.

I could finally relax a little bit. I'd already learned that I could never completely relax in a home that is far from childproof, with only a few toys I've managed to bring. I was relieved to see the ExerSaucer my mother picked up from the children's consignment center so I could put Tyler in when I needed a minute. With Brandon, I needed hawk eyes to make sure he didn't find a permanent marker and do to their walls what he'd done to ours.

But for two weeks I could eat my parents' cooking, sleep late while my mother fed the boys in the morning, and escape to the pool to tan by myself when they napped. It wasn't a luxury spa vacation, but for me it was pretty close.

WHERE DID YOU GET THEM FROM?

Hey, Gertrude!" I shouted, happy to see my swimming buddy from the last time I was here.

My parents live in a fifty-five-and-over condo, and the best part about it are the two large swimming pools. Instead of partying with college students in Mexico for vacation, I hung out with Betsy, Marty, and Harriet at the senior pool in Clearwater, Florida. I didn't mind at all. As a writer, I loved hearing all the stories they had to tell as we soaked in the water. While most of the men and women were lovely, I did have a few uncomfortable encounters with the seniors when it came to my Afro-Latino boys. One lady would not let Brandon pet her dog even though others petted him all the time.

"Do you still love your grandkids," she asked my mom later, "even though they're black?"

Another woman, who was genuinely sweet to the boys and me, invited me to her house. When I asked about two long, thin chairs, which looked ancient, she said, "Oh, those are slave chairs, honey," in her heavy southern accent. "Got them at a yard sale. That's where the house slaves would sit. 'Cause, you know, they didn't want them sitting on their furniture." I don't know if she understood the look on my face.

"They're so cute! I love their curly hair!" said another lady with a large sun hat.

"Thank you."

"Where'd you get them from?" she asked.

"I'm sorry, what?"

"The boys—what country? Where did you get them from?"

I looked at Brandon and Tyler, happily splashing around. Their suntans were glowing over their already bronzed skin.

"From my vagina," I wanted to say, but instead I smiled and said, "They're mine."

SLOPPY EATER

Tyler looked at the slice of chocolate frosted cake for a moment, and then dove in headfirst. My father was mortified. While my father enjoyed seeing us, his OCD was never thrilled by the mess that came with the territory.

"Why don't you feed it to him?" he pleaded.

"This is more fun," I said. I loved watching the boys explore their food. It wasn't just part of their development, it was hilarious.

He mumbled something to my mother, shaking his head, then scurried for a small towel from the kitchen.

"Here," he said, tucking part of it into Tyler's shirt. "So he doesn't dirty his shirt."

I laughed. "It was dirty five minutes after I put it on."

Tyler took a pause from massaging cake into his hair and ripped the towel off his chest. It landed on the floor. My father used it to clean bits of chocolate frosting and yellow cake from the kitchen tiles. I wanted to tell him it made more sense to wait until Tyler was done, but I left it alone.

Before Mami lifted him out of the chair for a bath, I took pictures of his chocolate massacre to send to Gavin. I cleaned up the mess and my father joined in. But as I watched him clean the crevices of the high chair with a Q-tip, I thought, *Maybe I'll leave our little exercises in sensory development to our place.*

FINANCES

B ack at home the stress over finances began to build.

The bills were late, and I was even paying some of them with my credit card. I had no choice. I sat at the table sorting through the mail; the red overdue marks on many of the bills made me nauseous.

"I want milk," Brandon asked, snapping me out of my mini depression.

I went to the fridge and poured him a cup. "Thank you, Mama," he said in his sweet voice.

"You're welcome, baby." I sighed.

Tyler crawled over to me and pulled on my leg for me to pick him up. I sat with him and buried my fingertips in his curly hair. He looked at me and smiled. His two deep dimples, two tiny teeth, and huge brown eyes penetrated my heart. "I'm sorry, baby boy," I said with a knot in my throat. I felt like a failure. I wanted to give them more.

My father's words echoed in my ear.

"I'm sorry I couldn't give you more. I wanted to give you so much more." It was something he'd said more than once when I was growing up. If he could, he would have bought my sister and me a house, given us enough money to see the world and savings to keep us secure for the rest of our lives. I understood now the regret in his words, but I also recalled my response. "Papi," I would say, hugging him tight and kissing his cheeks. "You've given me more than you will ever know. The love that you and Mami have given me makes me rich in ways that money could never satisfy. You've given me everything I need and I love you so much." Tyler touched my face and woke me from my daze as Brandon climbed up behind me to give me a big hug. I pressed my cheek on his head, which was resting on my shoulder as Tyler snuggled into my chest. *It's enough,* I told myself, knowing it had always been enough for me. *My love is more than enough.*

LULLABIES

Tyler was back in the hospital for RSV again, and they had us both in isolation. Gavin walked into the room that evening, and Tyler and I both lit up at seeing him.

"Dada," Tyler said, reaching out his arms. I was happy he'd come; I had spent the whole day alone with Tyler, worried about his breathing, keeping him occupied with Cheerios and cartoons on my computer. He'd just started taking wobbly steps and wanted down from my chair and the crib-with-a-roof I called baby jail.

"Oh, good, you brought the mats!" I said excitedly and began connecting them together on the floor immediately. Tyler looked into his daddy's eyes as Gavin spoke to him gently, waiting for the mats to be laid out.

"Okay, baby," I said. "Now you can walk around."

Gavin and I sat on the mat with him, playing with his toys.

"What did the doctor say?" he asked.

"His levels are normal now, but they have to keep a close eye," I said, extending a bowl of dry Cheerios to Tyler. "And I think he's getting a little ear infection, because he keeps rubbing his ear."

"He'll be all right," he said.

Tyler took a handful of Cheerios and brought them over to Gavin. He adored his father, and always gravitated toward him when he was in the room. I was happy for Tyler that Gavin could come.

"Thank you for sharing," Gavin said, putting some in his mouth.

I was relieved not to be alone, to have someone to share the experience with and calm my fears. Gavin took out his guitar and played beautiful and soothing music for Tyler. I lay back on my makeshift bed and closed my eyes. The guitar and my husband's presence made me feel safe. I could rest now and breathe easier, and I prayed that Tyler would continue to breathe easier, too.

FAMILY BAND

Days after Tyler was discharged, Gavin plugged in his electric guitar and played the blues. Tyler marched in circles near him, blowing into a silver harmonica, while Brandon sat at the mini drum set Evelyn bought him and banged the sticks on the snare.

"Yeah, yeah," Gavin encouraged Tyler. "Go, Tyler. Play that harp!"

Brandon banged the sticks wildly.

"Hit it like this, Bran Bran," he said, nodding his head to the right beat. Brandon followed.

I put the dishrag down and joined the band, singing made-up lyrics.

"Ain't got my goldfish," I sang. "Ain't got my goldfish anymore."

Gavin joined in on the vocals, and we sang together.

"Said ain't got my goldfish, ain't got my goldfish anymore."

I'm not sure what the neighbors thought. But our little band was music to my ears.

SEXY MAMA

I walked out of the dressing room and looked at myself in the three-way mirror. I was in shock. *I look good,* I thought to myself in disbelief. *Dare I even say sexy?* It had been a long time since I'd felt this way. Between my two pregnancies almost back to back and months of breast-feeding, my body hadn't felt like my own in quite a while. I stood there, no longer a house for a growing baby, no longer a nourishment center. Tyler was now completely on formula and solids. I could burn the ugly, stained breast-feeding bras and maybe buy some cute ones in different colors, perhaps a little lace. I no longer had to eat my veggies or skip the fudge brownie, but as I smiled at my reflection I thought, *Maybe I'll keep watching what I eat—for me this time.*

My hair had stopped falling out, and had I even started my monthly lady days again, something I'd never imagined I'd be happy to have back in my life. But it was a sign that things were falling back into place. I stood in front of that mirror for a long time. I twirled around. I put on a pair of heels. I played with my hair: half up, half down, a neat little bun, loose and crazy. The price tag kept tickling my arm as if telling me a decision had to be made. The dress was pricier than I would have liked it to be, but I made my way to the counter with a smile anyway. It was more than just a dress; it was a welcome-back party for the body that finally felt like my own once again.

TYLER'S FIRST BIRTHDAY

I spent hours the night before making Tyler's bug cupcakes out of M&M's and frosting. There were caterpillars, bumblebees, spiders, and ants. It was perfect for my little boy's birthday picnic. When I opened the box the next morning I learned an important lesson about refrigerating icing and chocolate.

"My bugs!" I whined, trying to fix the mess of green-grass frosting and melted M&M's, which had all slid down the hills of each cupcake.

"Nobody cares," Diane said, trying to make me feel better. "As long as they taste good!"

I greeted each guest as they joined the growing tapestry of blankets in Central Park, and groaned about my cupcakes as I kissed them hello.

"What great weather you got!" my friend Laura said.

"I know! It's such a beautiful day!" I agreed, excited by the spring-like weather on an autumn day.

Tyler slept through most of the festivities, but the guests and their kids had a great time eating, playing, lying about, and chatting. I went from blanket to blanket talking with each guest as Gavin sat under a tree farther away, plucking at his guitar.

"Isn't this his son's party, too?" my friend's husband asked. He chuckled but shook his head and patted my shoulder.

"Yeah, I know," I said with a smile and waved my hand to dismiss the very idea of telling Gavin to mingle with our guests. I'd learned to let it go, although his behavior still embarrassed me.

For Christmas in Florida, he'd locked himself away in one of the bedrooms playing chess on his computer.

"Where's your husband?" some of the guests asked.

"Oh, he's not feeling well," I'd lied.

My anger didn't make him come out of the room and only created more tension.

"He's happy playing his guitar," I said now, "so I'm just going to leave it alone."

Tyler woke up crying. I picked him up, wiped his tears, and pushed away the sweaty curls pressed to his temples. We put him in the middle of a giant, colorful parachute, and this cheered him up. He smiled and laughed with his two bottom bunny teeth as we shook the ends of the fabric, creating waves of red, blue, and green all around him.

We pushed candles into my cupcake disaster and sang "Happy Birthday," gave out goody bags filled with candy, toys, and mini bubbles. Then Gavin, Brandon, Tyler, and I followed Gavin's cousin to a pretty bridge to take pictures—one of the last family portraits we'd smile for.

FAMILY RESTAURANT

It was just the boys and me again, but we were cooped up in the apartment all day and I was going stir-crazy. Tyler was running a fever, so there were no playdates, no adult conversations. By late afternoon, after his fever broke, I took them for a walk. I hadn't eaten much all day and wanted to treat myself.

"We're going out for dinner," I declared. I piled them in the stroller and took the elevator down.

As we arrived at the restaurant I struggled through the narrow door. This was a mistake, I immediately realized. The place was packed, and there was obviously no room for a double stroller. People sat in large groups laughing and eating with their families and friends as I awkwardly tried to maneuver the wide stroller back out the door. The sound of multiple conversations faded as we left, and the return to silence made me cry. I felt alone. I wandered aimlessly, looking for something to eat, tears falling uncontrollably, hands too occupied with pushing the heavy stroller to wipe them. I wished I could be in that restaurant with people I loved. I wanted them to fight over who holds Tyler; I wanted to snuggle into my father's arm and laugh at my cousin's stories. But everyone I loved was either too far away or too busy with their own lives to be a part of mine. I missed the constant affection and commotion I grew up with. I never imagined this would be my life, my children's life. I felt alone.

I found an almost empty barbecue grill. The three of us sat there, Tyler massaging his gums with corn on the cob, Brandon eating butter straight from the tiny container.

"Yummy," he said in a deep, raspy voice, obviously trying to be funny. Tyler looked up from his corn and giggled. Brandon did it again. This time we all cracked up.

I wasn't surrounded by the large family I so dearly missed; but as I ate and laughed with this small, newer family of my own, it made the heartache a little easier to bear.

DRUNK WHITE GIRL

Listen to this drunk-white-girl nonsense." Gavin laughed, showing me a message on his phone. Amused and disturbed, I listened to a slurred proclamation of love for Gavin. "But I'm not gonna do it," she muddled. "I'm not gonna be a home wrecker."

With all our issues, the one I never worried about was Gavin being unfaithful.

"That's just tacky," he'd said, back when we were friends. "What's the point in being in a relationship with someone if you're going to do that?"

Days later, we were at his Christmas party for the gym, where I used to work as well. It was a great night. I snuggled into his arm, we danced, held hands, and laughed with friends. I was happy the two of us were enjoying each other, especially since he would be leaving for Texas again soon. It was time for the annual boxing tournament with the military, and he would be gone for two to three months. As up and down as we'd been for the last few years, I knew I'd miss him; and I treasured this fun evening together when things felt good between us. But, as amazing as our evening was, that was the beginning of our end.

⌒

"I checked out that new cheesecake place I was telling you about," he said as we were filling our plates at the party buffet.

"Oh yeah? How was it?"

"The cheesecake was really good."

"Who did you go with?" I asked.

"Jen," he said casually.

"Jen?" I paused for a moment. "The drunk-white-girl Jen? The one who's in love with you?"

"Yes."

"Why?"

"What do you mean, why? Why not? I still have to work with her. And after all"—he chuckled as he said this—"I *did* let her down."

I tried to explain, careful not to sound jealous, that hanging out with her would make her think there was hope. But he brushed it off as "not a big deal."

"It doesn't matter if she's interested in me. The point is, I'm not interested in her."

I let it go. He had never given me a reason to be jealous, and I wasn't going to start now.

⌒

I fell asleep with Brandon one night, days after the party. I woke up after midnight twisted uncomfortably in the tiny bed. I kissed each of my babies, straightened my aching back, then shuffled out of the room. Gavin was not home. I called him. No answer. My phone rang awhile later. It was him.

"Hey, sorry. I didn't hear my phone—the music was too loud." He said, "I went to listen to music at B.B. King's with a co-worker."

"Oh, okay, no worries," I said, then added—as a joke—"What co-worker? Jen?"

"Yes."

CHESS

When Gavin came home that night he tried to wake me up. Why was I mad? Why had I hung up on him?

I didn't get up. I had no energy to have this conversation.

He left early in the morning, before Tyler's crying woke me up.

I was justified. I was angry and I was justified! I paced through the day, writing valid points on scraps of paper between changing diapers and making peanut-butter-and-jelly sandwiches. *This is wrong! But he'll find a way to make it sound like I'm crazy. He always does,* I thought. I was a weak opponent in his chess game. There was no winning—ever. But this? This was checkmate. It had to be. Because there was no way he could justify how wrong this was.

The chessboard was set for when he came home.

I moved first.

"These are dates!" I yelled. "You are going out on dates with a woman who has feelings for you!"

He calmly countered, "It's not a date if I have no feelings for her."

I moved another piece.

"It doesn't look right! You are disrespecting me as your wife!"

He paused before his next move.

"That's the problem with the institution of marriage. It's all a show for the benefit of others. You can't do this, you can't do that, because of how it looks. I have never given you a reason to be jealous."

The man who barely spoke to me now had a lot to say. As far as he was concerned, I was insecure and ridiculous—and it wasn't a good look on me. I sat there silenced as he went on and on. I had no more moves to play, but he had one more.

"I want a divorce," he said. "I already looked into it."

Checkmate.

SINGLE MOM

"I should be on Prozac,
but I'm on prayer instead."

MY HOUSEKEEPER IS ON VACATION

I'm so annoyed right now!" a fellow mom grumbled at an open play space. "My nanny called in sick today! This couldn't have come at a worse time! My husband is on a business trip and my housekeeper is on vacation!"

Her mellow daughter sat quietly nearby, playing with a doll. Brandon and Tyler were running around in circles, yelling louder than all the kids combined.

I forced a smile as she complained, fighting the urge to cry, fighting the impulse to shake her and scream louder than my kids, "What do you know about suffering? Your husband is coming back—mine isn't!" *How dare she complain,* I thought. *She has nothing to complain about!* I watched her lips move as my rage toward her swirled inside me like a gust of wind. At least she had a nanny! I could never afford someone to help me with the boys. A housekeeper? I could only dream of a housekeeper to clean the mess that was waiting for me at home.

"Excuse me," I said, getting up, afraid of having a meltdown in front of these women with their perfect lives. I wrestled my two toddlers into their coats, then shoved my massive double stroller through the snow. I had never appreciated the cold more than at these moments. The sting of the winter air continually slapped me out of my despair, which persisted in layering over me like a grave. It reminded me I was still alive and needed to keep going. The boys still needed fresh diapers, peanut-butter-and-jelly sandwiches, someone to soothe them out of their tantrums. They still needed a childhood, and I still needed to be their mother.

When their sleepy little heads rested on their pillows, I'd caress their curls until their eyes finally closed. Then I'd tiptoe out of their room and crumple onto the floor.

GOD HAS GIVEN YOU A VOICE

I don't know how to make it through January," I sobbed into the phone to Diane. "And then after January, I still have to get through February!"

Every day I felt hollow—pieced together with a delicate outer shell, weighed down with burdens too great for my fragile frame to hold. "And I'm trying, Diane, I'm trying to hold it together for the boys, but every day it feels like it's getting harder to do."

My sister drove down to the city. Three of my cousins came, too. They sat with me quietly as I cried, like one does for a grieving widow at a funeral.

They prayed with me, encouraged me, and even made me laugh.

"I know you want to crumble into a ball and disappear right now," my cousin Elizabeth said, "but you can't allow this to defeat you. That's not what you were made for. God has given you a voice. You are going to heal through music. Even if it doesn't make any sense to you, you have to praise him through the pain."

I thanked her for her words, but the last thing I wanted to do was sing.

GLOW

The boys slept as I rolled them through the narrow aisles of the grocery store. I placed milk, bread, and a few other items we needed on the awning of the stroller. I had to be careful about how much I bought. Gavin said he would continue to pay rent for a while, but money had already been tight before he left. Soon we would do our taxes. I hoped we would get a big enough refund to live on while I figured out what to do next. I placed the items on the counter and reached into my bag to find my debit card. The checkout girl looked at me and smiled as she scanned my groceries.

"You are just glowing!" she said.

I shot my head up and looked at her in shock.

"Who, me?"

"Yes," she said, nodding her head. "Seriously, it's like, radiating."

"That's funny," I said. "It must be all the prayers people are sending my way. I should be on Prozac, but I guess I'm on prayer instead." There was no one behind me, so I filled her in on what was going on. I wasn't shy about telling anyone what I was going through, and it didn't matter if we'd just met. I couldn't hold it in. There was a need in me to tell people what was happening—as if they could say something that would cure the wound.

The checkout girl handed me my bag and I placed it over the stroller handlebars.

"I'll send out prayers for you, too," she said.

I smiled and went back home.

The snow was coming down hard now. It had been snowing for

days and the amount of energy it took to get us all dressed and out of the house felt enormous. I wished the boys hadn't fallen asleep in the stroller. That meant I couldn't rest with them.

I rolled them into the apartment and quietly put the groceries away. I tiptoed to the couch and lay down. My body felt heavy on the cushions. My eyelids closed. But just before I fell asleep, Brandon and Tyler woke up.

I CAN'T DO THIS

N o!" Brandon shouted, pushing away the plate of spaghetti he'd asked for just a few minutes ago. It was the second dish he'd demanded, only to turn it away. Tyler, never finicky with his food, shoved a fistful of pasta and broccoli into his mouth. His head was draped in spaghetti strings and his face covered in sauce.

"What is it?" I asked desperately as Brandon threw himself on the floor, crying. "What do you want?"

Brandon kept screaming while Tyler smiled, swirling his hand in his plate. "Mo bah-kiki peeze!"

I emptied the last bit of broccoli onto his plate and tossed the small pot into the sink. It sat balanced over a mountain of dirty dishes. I couldn't keep up with the mess. The laundry was pouring over in baskets and onto the floor, along with scattered bits of Cheerios, toys, and crayons. What was the point? I was sleep deprived and moved nonstop all day, but no matter how hard I worked, I was still drowning in a growing chaos.

I don't want to be a mother today! I screamed in my head, wanting to throw Brandon's plate of spaghetti across the room. I didn't. It would only add to the mess. I reached down to pick up my crying son and, as if on cue, he leaned forward and vomited all over my arms and the dining room floor.

⌒

For a week it was like the bubonic plague. All three of us had caught the bug, and it taught me new levels of exhaustion. I consoled my sick boys and washed vomit off bedsheets, while I myself could keep nothing down.

"I can't do this!" I prayed out loud in a panic. "Lord, please help me. I can't do this anymore!"

The fevers broke, the vomiting and diarrhea stopped, but the misery and hopelessness remained. It followed me everywhere. Only the boys could snap me out of it once in a while with their sweet little faces and oblivious joy.

SING

My cousin's words echoed. "God has given you a voice. You are going to heal through music. Even if it doesn't make any sense to you, you have to praise him through the pain."

I spoke to the music director at church, and we set a date for me to do special music.

A week and a half later, I sat at the piano in my church. The congregation, most of whom knew my situation, sat hushed as they waited for me to sing. I took a breath and began to play the chords. I could feel the music doing something inside of me, whirling through with an indescribable peace and power. I raised my head and sang the first few lines of the song I'd written. Writing the words was the first part of my release, but as my voice filled the church, I could feel all of the hurt lifting out from inside of me and escaping with each note I sang.

At the end of the service I got hugs from so many.

"You made me cry," one said.

"You touched my heart," said another.

"That was a beautiful duet," said my friend Dominique, who was sitting with Tyler while I sang. "Because this little one right here was singing right along with you."

⌒

I filled my home with praise music. The music and words became life-lines, lifting me slowly from under. One song became my mantra. I would play it over and over. It sang:

> I'll praise you in this storm, and I will lift my hands.
> You are who you are, no matter where I am.
> And every tear I've cried, you hold in your hands.
> You've never left my side.
> And though my heart is torn.
> I will praise you in this storm.

VALENTINE'S DAY

Gavin was still in Texas when he left a message for me on Valentine's Day.

"I know you might not want to hear this right now, but I just wanted to tell you that I love you and I care about you and I'm going to be there for you. It's just that our relationship is going to be different, that's all."

I listened to the message in the drugstore as I picked up another large bag of diapers. The store was covered in pink and red; large heart balloons with curly strings, boxes of chocolate candy rimmed in lace, and teddy bears big and small waited on counters to be gifts for women in love.

⌒

I waited until the boys were napping to call him back.

"Hi," I said.

"Hey," he said sweetly.

"So, what you're saying is, we get to be friends now?"

"Yes. There's no reason for us not to be."

I breathed out, smiling in disbelief.

"Friendship," I said, and then the rest poured out of my heart, seemingly without a breath. "My love for you came from the most beautiful friendship I've ever had. And the moment you married me you took that friendship away. You were anything but a friend to me throughout our marriage. You had no compassion for me, you didn't care about me, you treated me like I didn't matter and neither did my feelings. And, as miserable as you made me for three years, I held on to my love for you and my hope that the man who was once my best friend in the whole world, the one who treated me so wonderfully, would come back to me, but you never did. And now you say good-bye to our marriage with a wink and a smile, like it's no big deal, without even trying to make it work. And after all that pain you caused throughout the years and especially that last week before you left for Texas, you want to be my *buddy*? Well, you know what, Gavin? You don't get to have my friendship. You don't get to have any more of my heart than I've already given you. Because I gave it *all* to you, and you destroyed it like it was nothing to you. I can't trust you with any part of me anymore. Not even in friendship. You have hurt me more than you will ever know, and I want as little to do with you as possible. I know you have to be in my life to some extent because of the boys, and I want you in their lives. I want them to have a father. But that's all. I have to give my heart to God now, and let him heal the damage you've done, and I will heal. I will be just fine. And maybe in time after I've healed from all of this, we can have some sort of a friendship. But for now, you get nothing."

TOO MUCH BROKEN

He didn't stay in Texas as long as he'd expected. He didn't make it far in the competition and was back in New York City by the end of February.

"Daddy!" the boys squealed when they saw him for the first time since he'd left. Gavin wrapped his arms around them and picked them up as they giggled in delight. I wanted him to wrap his arms around me like that, too, but, at the same time, I didn't want him to touch me at all.

"Hi." He smiled.

I nodded. "Hi."

Gavin and I had business to take care of. We had to discuss money, file our taxes, and talk about taking turns with the boys.

We sat at the kitchen table and spoke like business partners. I thought about the day in Central Park, after we'd broken up for the first time, how we'd kissed on the cheek and spoken about how our breakup made sense, and how it had ended with Gavin kissing the tears on my cheek. And while I had no expectations of history repeating itself, by the end of our talk at the kitchen table he was kissing the tears on my cheek again.

We made love over and over. It was the best sex we'd had in all our years together—not guilty fornication sex, not insecure pregnant sex, not I-don't-think-he-loves-me-anymore sex, just indescribable, intoxicating sex. And although I held on to him for dear life that night, I knew there was too much broken to be fixed.

The next morning we spoke about ways to make it work.

"Let's just let each other be who we are" was his solution. But I didn't understand how I wasn't already doing this.

"Let's see a marriage counselor" was mine. But he didn't understand how a stranger could help us.

I wasn't willing to jump back into our marriage so soon without help. The wound was too deep, and I no longer trusted him with my damaged heart. I needed to move toward healing, with or without him.

WHAT A BEAUTIFUL FAMILY

We stood in line at the supermarket. Gavin held Brandon, who was shoving a doughnut in his mouth. Tyler was peacefully sleeping in the stroller in front of me.

"What a beautiful family," said an older woman, whose eyes sparkled with sweetness toward us.

"Thank you," we said.

We were still like a family, but we weren't. It was just like the message he'd left for me on Valentine's Day: "Our relationship is going to be different, that's all."

The declaration I had so vehemently protested.

Gavin spent time at the house, we shopped for food, we cooked together, we played with the boys, he slept over. We were the family we used to be, minus the tension and the sex.

"This is strange," my friend said when she came over to visit. "I mean, you're either together or you're not. You guys are just playing house."

I didn't know how to answer her. It didn't make enough sense for me to give a valid explanation. "That's just how we are handling things at the moment," I finally said.

We celebrated Brandon's third birthday and smiled for family pictures. We took the boys to the playground, watched TV, and laughed together on the couch just like a family, but not.

THREE

Brandon and Tyler were cranky and due for a nap. I put them in their beds, but they kept coming out of the room.

I looked over at Gavin to ask for help. He was smiling at his laptop. He typed, waited, then chuckled under his breath. I felt my stomach turn.

"Come on, guys," I said, leading them back to the room. "Nap time."

"I'm going to take a shower," Gavin announced through the closed bedroom door.

"Okay," I said.

I waited to hear the water running, then walked out of the bedroom and into the living room. My heart began a drumroll in my chest. *That wasn't just a regular smile,* I thought. Part of me didn't want to know what he was smiling at, but the other part walked right over to his laptop and clicked the touchpad. The drumroll in my chest grew louder and stronger as I read a dialogue between him and another girl.

"Mami," Brandon said, coming out of the room yet again. His tiny voice snapped me away from the screen, her pretty picture, the hearts at the ends of her sentences.

I didn't respond to my son. Instead I raged toward the bathroom and banged on the door. "Get out!" I screamed. "Get out of my house!"

The water shut off and he came out in a towel demanding to know what was going on. I told him what I'd seen.

"I want you out of here!" I screamed wildly, cursing him and pacing the floor.

"Get *out!*"

"You and I are not together anymore," he said calmly, the cool in his voice making me sound like even more of a raging lunatic than already I did. "I've simply moved on."

Tyler came out of the room, too, and started crying, lifting his arms for me to pick him up.

"You just made love to me three weeks ago!" I yelled. "You told me you loved me three weeks ago, and now you're moving on?"

Gavin gathered his things, relaxed and unruffled. "Three weeks, three months, three years…it's never enough time for the other person who hasn't moved on!"

Tyler was wailing now. Brandon joined in, too.

"Oh, is *that* what I'm supposed to be doing here?" I screamed. "Moving on with someone else?"

He gave me a smug "You're pathetic" smile and walked out the door, leaving the three of us howling uncontrollable tears.

RED PENCIL

The money from our income tax was running low, and I had no backup plan for when it ran out. I was a stay-at-home mom. I hadn't written a proposal since I'd met Gavin, and the very thought of having time to write and get published again seemed unreachable. The money I'd earn from teaching gymnastics would never be enough to cover all my bills in addition to the hefty cost of child care in New York City. I was still doing music classes in the park, and knew I had to boost up attendance before my bank accounts dropped to nothing.

One night I laid out all my colored pencils on the table, and one by one made new business cards by hand. I drew a tree with an acoustic guitar as its trunk and a bright blue sky. I lettered my information in bright red. I couldn't afford to order new cards.

The boys were down for the night and, as usual, the stress from the day and my heartache poured out of me after dark. My despair had reached a height I would never have imagined feeling.

The tip of the red pencil broke, and I got a straight-edged razor from the bathroom to sharpen it, like my father used to do when I was a little girl.

…The pain I was carrying felt too big to fit in my body, almost as if it were pushing out from inside, my skin ready to explode. …

I placed the razor on the pencil and watched bits of wood and red-colored lead scatter on the table.

...My body heaved in sobs. I was so tired of crying. I was so tired of feeling this pain. There was no relief. ...

I watched the blade easily slice through the wood. I thought of my sister's friend who used to cut herself with blades like these when she was a teenager. She said it released the emotional pain. I never understood the sense in that, but I did now. The pain pushed out from inside me like never before, but there was nowhere for it to go. It was just building and building. I was ready to burst.

...I shaved the pencil quickly. It was already sharpened but I kept going, contemplating, weeping, heaving. I flicked the blade to the flesh of my arm. I pressed down, creating a shallow trench in my skin, not deep enough to draw blood.

If you do this, I thought, *you have crossed a line.*

I thought of my little boys sleeping in their room and lifted the blade from my arm. The next day I made an appointment to see a therapist.

SPRINKLERS

It was the first day the sprinklers came on in Central Park. Summer was finally here. I listened to the water splashing on the ground, watched my boys' faces as they ran under the cold stream of water, smelled the sunscreen still on my hands from slathering their arms and chubby bellies. I took in the moment with a breath, as if it were the first time I'd been able to breathe in a long time. That was the longest winter of my life. I thought of that phone call with Diane in January, when I'd been wondering how I could possibly get through the month. Blind with grief, I couldn't imagine a day where pain wasn't a constant companion. All I could do was pray to get through each day, sing through the hurt, kiss and cuddle my sweet boys. I wasn't angry at God. Not this time. I'd already done the angry-at-God thing years before I met Gavin, and it did nothing for me. This time I held on to God with all my might. Throughout the long winter days, and even into that late spring when things got worse, I could feel his spirit walking beside me, grieving with me and for me, leading me slowly to a brighter day. It was a long, painful road, but as I stood there with cool water under my bare feet, watching my boys enjoying the start of a long-awaited summer, I knew I was almost there.

GRAFFITI CHURCH

It was an unknown caller, and I almost didn't pick it up.

"Hello," I said with a bit of annoyance, certain it was a salesperson bugging me about products and services I couldn't afford.

"Karen? Hi. It's Pastor Taylor from East Seventh Baptist Church," he said.

East Seventh was better known as Graffiti Church. It was on the Lower East Side. They'd rented space from our Spanish-speaking congregation when my father was a pastor in Manhattan. They had outgrown the small storefront on Seventh Street and used our basement for Sunday service. When I saw the pastor's wife walk in wearing ripped jeans, I fell in love with them. It was a stark contrast to my church, whose members thought women should wear only dresses on a Sunday morning. I would sneak out of Spanish service to listen to the tall, white pastor whose head almost touched the short ceiling.

I was a teenager, confused about my faith, and his simple words helped restore it. I enjoyed giving out sandwiches to homeless men and women with them; I worked as a counselor in their summer program and looked forward to their annual retreats in Pennsylvania. I got a kick out of their name, which came from actual graffiti on their storefront in the 1970s. They tried to paint over it again and again, then finally just added their own graffiti with words of love and encouragement for the community.

~

"Oh, wow," I gasped into the phone. I hadn't heard from him in a long time. It had been well over ten years since I'd left my father's church to worship at another closer to home. "Hi, Pastor Taylor!"

"I'm so happy you picked up. I was sure your number had changed after all these years," he said.

He explained that their current children's director was about to leave, and they needed to fill the position.

"We thought of you and all the great work you did at your church with the kids. Would you be interested in interviewing for the job?"

I couldn't believe what I was hearing. The money in my account from our tax return was dwindling. I knew I'd have to figure out a way to support the boys, but I didn't even know where to start. I was in denial; I wasn't even looking for work. And, out of nowhere, this opportunity was simply hand delivered. It would be a salaried job, which paid more than enough for the cost of living, plus child care. I only had to be in the office Monday through Wednesday. Thursday I'd work from home, and Sunday while I was in church counted as a workday, too.

"I'd love to interview!" I said, then made arrangements for the next step.

I hung up the phone in awe. "Thank you, Lord," I said, still shocked by the phone call. "Thank you."

A BLESSING, NOT A CURSE

I got the job!" I screamed over the phone to my mother. She was the first person I'd called after officially being offered the position. The financial burden I'd carried after my separation was finally lifted. I could get out of debt; the application for food stamps didn't have to be mailed. I would start in September, just a month away, and they'd give me a generous stipend for August as I prepared for the position.

I hung up the phone just before I opened the door to my apartment.

"Mami!" Brandon and Tyler screamed as I peeked my head through the door. They dropped what they were doing and came running over to me as they always did when I walked through the door. I dropped to the floor, wrapping them both in my arms, kissing their chubby cheeks. Their overwhelming love for me on their tiny faces suddenly made my excitement about employment disappear. I would no longer be with them all day, every day, showering them with kisses, creating fun activities at home, watching them play until they were breathless at the playground. I could no longer take them to interesting places like museums, free concerts, and beautiful city gardens. Now I had to think of child-care options. Would their new caretakers be patient, teach them new things, play with them? Suddenly I became bitter about my situation. The needs of my family were taking me away from them. My position at Graffiti also meant saying goodbye to the church family I'd been a part of for twelve years. Sunday mornings would be part of my workweek, so I wouldn't even be able to visit them. Every person I still had left in my life was going to be taken away from me.

"Hi, Mami," I said when my mother called me the next day.

Her excitement contrasted with my emotions.

"I was just telling Betty about your new job offer," she said, practically giddy over the phone. "Isn't that just amazing how God works? I mean, the way he has met your need just at the right time is incredible!"

As my mother spoke I began to smile, and slowly the gratitude came back. This new path, I realized, was completely God's doing. The job came looking for me before I began job hunting. The position was something I had passion for and knew I could do well. It was exactly what I needed, when I needed it. This was a hand-wrapped blessing from God. It was not a curse. It was a new beginning filled with the promise of wonderful things to come.

YOU FEED THE GOATS, NOT THE PEOPLE

Here, Brandon," I said, pouring goat-food pellets into his little hand. "Go feed the goat."

Before I started my new job, I wanted to give my boys a great summer. Our days were filled with fun adventures at pools, playgrounds, zoos, beaches, and sprinklers. They enjoyed ice cream and movies, sand and water balloons. For our excursions in the city, we'd leave after breakfast and come back in the afternoon for lunch, then a bath and a cool nap in the air-conditioned bedroom. After we were completely refreshed, we'd go back outside for more. For the most part, I treasured every day with my babies. But of course there were the days where the two of them would gang up on me and drive me bonkers. My sweet Zen-baby, Tyler, had transformed into quite the terror. Two months shy of his second birthday, he was already the very definition of terrible twos.

"Tyler, no!" He was trying to feed a goat pellet to a woman sitting nearby. His hand was almost touching her mouth. "You feed the goats, not the people."

The child kept me on my toes: he tried to flush the toilet-paper roll down the toilet, sprinkled the whole container of baby powder on the floor, chewed crayons like chewing tobacco and pooped rainbows.

Bedtime was a nightmare. With the crib finally retired and replaced with a new big-boy bed, my "nighttime me-time" was over. Instead of kissing them sweetly good night then retiring to the living room to unwind with TV and chocolate, I was in and out of the room chasing them back to bed. Brandon, who had never gotten out of his bed at night, was now Tyler's faithful accomplice. They'd climb furniture, play with their toys, empty out the sock drawer, strip naked and cover their bodies in stickers.

Once they'd found and broken a pen, and when I walked in on them they were covered in ink—along with the quilts.

～

Gavin would keep them for a weekend at least once a month.

"Here you go!" I'd say on Friday, shooing them out the door toward him. I'd finally have some peace of mind. But by Saturday evening their absence would pull at my heart. I'd miss snuggling next to them under the covers, listening to Brandon's silly stories complete with sound effects. I'd miss Tyler's warm cuddles, his kisses all over my face, and his sweet declarations of love. "I wuv oo, Mama. I wuv oo."

On Sunday, when they were running into my arms, that little missing piece in my soul that disappeared when they were gone would go right back where it belonged.

GROWN-UP STUFF

There were bagels, almonds, hummus, and juicy dates on the table for my first staff meeting at Graffiti.

There were no Cheerios in the mix, no one was twisting on the floor having a tantrum; I wasn't picking up clothing and toys from the floor. I was in a room full of only adults and I couldn't have been more excited about it. I'd never realized how starved for adult companionship I was until we sat around that table ready to tackle serious, grown-up stuff. I could use my professional voice, not my baby voice.

I learned that before logistics and calendaring, each week someone would bring a devotion—a story, a Bible verse that spoke to his or her heart, or just a life lesson learned throughout the week.

"I wanted to share Isaiah 43:2 with you today," my co-worker Carmen said as she opened her Bible to the Old Testament. "It reads: *'When you pass through the waters, I will be with you; and when you pass through the rivers, they will not sweep over you. When you walk through the fire, you will not be burned; the flames will not set you ablaze.'*"

The lump in my throat had already emerged with the verse, and it only grew as she spoke. She was a survivor of cancer and a number of other life experiences that should have left her dead. But here she was, this amazing woman with her strong, yet peaceful, voice that soothed my soul to its core. By the time they asked for prayer requests and got to me, I could barely get the words out of my mouth before I broke down in tears. So much for using my professional, grown-up voice.

For the first year at Graffiti, that was my healing room. I poured out my heart, my fears, my sadness, and my tears almost every week.

And that beautiful circle of leaders rallied around me, let me cry, prayed for me, and encouraged me through every step forward.

WEDNESDAY NIGHT MEAL

As I opened the door, the odor crawled up into my nose and settled in like a dying rat. I held my breath and zipped past the homeless men and women who sat at tables waiting to be fed. After a month as children's director, I now had to stay late for the next ten Wednesdays for Connections—meals and activities for our after-school children and their families. The lower level was where other adults, mostly homeless people, had Wednesday Night Meal, which ran year-round. That first evening, I had to make the dreaded stench-walk toward the resource room several times. The second time, I prepared myself with a deep breath and my feet ready to go double time. As I opened the door and took my first quick steps, something made me slow down. The pastor, with his tall stature and friendly face, greeted these men and women like old friends. *Poor Pastor,* I thought. *He has to bear the smell a little longer as he says hello and good-bye.* After I fumbled around in the resource room and collected what I needed, I went back out to zip past them again. The pastor was now sitting at one of the tables, talking and laughing with them, eating the same food. Suddenly I felt silly rushing. I overheard one of the men sharing a war story, and he had the pastor's full attention. By the third time, I didn't even hold my breath. I was getting used to the smell. The food was gone, the tables had been moved, and everyone sat in chairs forming a big circle. The pastor was leading a Bible study. I always thought of myself as a humble person with a servant's heart, but suddenly all I could see was my own filth of selfishness and self-righteousness. Feeling a bit ashamed, I gathered more supplies and walked slowly and quietly past the group. The pastor began to lead them in a familiar song and noticed me. "Oh, Karen has a great voice," he said with a smile. "Maybe she can help us." Their faces lit up as I sang, and when I finished, they let out the most exuberant round of applause I'd ever received. "Thank you," I said, grateful for more than their appreciation of the song. Their cheers felt like a wave of forgiveness cleansing the offensive odor of my guilt.

GRUMPY MAMI

I want yogurt, Mami! Mami, I want yogurt. Ma-ma-Mami, can I have some yogurt? Yooooogurt. Mami, I want yogurt?" This was a normal start to my morning. But on this particular day I was not in the mood.

"I heard you!" I snarled. "Now sit down and wait! Can't you see me getting it for you?" I mumbled under my breath and slapped spoonfuls of yogurt into a bowl. I was unusually tired and extremely annoyed at Gavin, who was supposed to watch them but didn't. Now I'd have to miss work and let the pile of responsibilities there continue to pile. I served them each a bowl of yogurt and shuffled over to the dirty clothes. At least I could get some stuff done here. As I sorted, Tyler found a paintbrush and began painting a giggling Brandon's face with his yogurt.

"What are you doing?" I huffed, reaching for a paper towel to clean Brandon's face. The rest of the day I could not get rid of my mean-Mami voice.

"Stop it!" "What did I say!" "No!" "Sit still so I can put on your shoe!" The more frustrated I became the more they did to push my buttons.

"Brandon! I said get down! Do you need a time-out?"

My son looked at me and began to laugh.

"Oh," I asked, getting really upset. "So you think that's funny?"

"No, I don't think that's funny," he said with a smile and a shrug. "I'm just happy, Mami. I'm happy and you're not."

I NEED YOU TO STOP CRYING

Hours before, I had been happily filling out forms for an extremely affordable home-care program for my boys. We were assigned to a place near our apartment, and they had assured me the woman was a sweetheart. Brandon and Tyler would be in her care for nine hours, five days a week; there'd be other children to play with, and they'd have snacks and two meals a day. I was beyond excited. Although Gavin was helping me take care of the boys, it wasn't with the consistency I needed for my job. The nanny I hired was amazing with the boys, but she was expensive. This kind of arrangement was exactly what I needed.

I pushed the stroller about five blocks from our apartment. This was going to be perfect!

I rang the doorbell and waited anxiously to meet the caregiver. The lady at the office had told me how sweet she was, and I couldn't wait to introduce her to the boys.

She opened the door slowly and invited me in. As I stood in the tiny apartment, my breath was completely taken from me. It was small, dark, crowded with furniture and old toys scattered everywhere. The atmosphere was heavy, depressing.

"Out," Tyler said tugging on the stroller straps.

I unbuckled them and the woman led me to the couch to sit down.

For a moment we didn't speak; I didn't know what to say. I watched the boys pick up toys from the ground. A toddler who was much younger than my active boys wobbled by with a sagging diaper. A baby lay restless in a playpen whining to herself.

"What do the kids do all day?" I managed.

She picked up the baby girl and watched my boys, who were already the loudest ones in the room.

"*Ellos juegan con los juguetes,*" she answered, saying they play with toys. She didn't speak English.

I wanted to ask if she took them outside, but before I could ask another question she made sure to tell me I'd be charged extra if I picked them up late. My kids looked like trapped animals in a small cage. I felt trapped, too. This was what I could afford. I opened my mouth to ask my question about going outside, and instead I began to cry. I tried to explain myself, but I could barely speak at all, let alone in Spanish. I scooped up the boys, put them in the double stroller, and headed for the door. "*Perdóname,*" I apologized, "*Yo no estoy…no puedo.*" I couldn't find the words and I could not stop crying. I resented Gavin for doing this to me—to our children.

꩜

My kids were quiet as I continued to sob, waiting for the elevator, exiting the building, walking down the street. "Mami," Brandon finally asked, "why are you crying?"

I stopped the stroller, knelt down to my three-year-old, and tried to explain what was wrong.

"Mami's crying because I love you guys so much!" I said, gasping for air. "And I'm trying to find someone to take care of you when I work. I want you to have fun and I wish I could just stay with you, but I can't."

He looked at me without blinking an eye. He almost looked annoyed.

"Mami," he said with the stern calmness of a parent, and repeated what his nanny would say to him when he was having a tantrum: "I need you to stop crying."

It was as if he'd slapped me square in the face.

We just stared at each other for a moment, then I wiped my tears and regained my composure.

I pushed the stroller away from that place, knowing I would never go back. It would work out. We'd be okay. I thanked God for reminding me through my little boy to be still and "know that I am God."

"Help me to trust you, Lord," I prayed.

I continued to pay for the nanny, whom I loved and trusted, until the nearby day care—the one with the sliding-scale payment system and the long waiting list—finally gave us a call.

TOY SALE

The annual toy sale at Graffiti was coming up, and the thought of being in charge of such a huge event gave me nightmares. Each year more than a hundred people would line up outside of the church, some arriving the night before to secure their spot. For a small donation to our children's program, families could choose from an array of new, donated items and walk out with a giant bag filled with several toys.

I arrived at six in the morning to finish setting up the different floors—one for waiting and Christmas caroling, one for shopping, another for counseling and prayer. I was in charge of more than fifty volunteers, and every final decision rested on my shoulders. How in the world was Graffiti putting so much trust in me? I could barely get my kids out in the morning, and they wanted me to delegate and run this whole show? It boggled my mind the trust Pastor Taylor had in me. He'd hired me, even when he knew the emotional state I was in. And anytime I showed doubt in our meetings he'd say, "You're Karen Valentin! You can do this."

We opened the doors and it began. Each person received a number, showed us proof of guardianship, and went downstairs to the waiting room.

"This woman doesn't have documentation," a volunteer said, pointing to an older woman.

"Ma'am, I'm sorry, but you'll have to go home to get it and come back."

"Hey," a man said, coming to her defense. "She's been waiting a long time."

"I understand that, sir," I replied, trying to remain professional and check my desire to just let her through. "But this is a rule that applies to all, and it wouldn't be fair to those who brought their documentation today. Unfortunately, people have taken advantage in the past, and we've had to set these regulations to serve the community better."

I had to face her disappointment and anger—and she was just one of many.

I ran down to the basement to call the first ten numbers to go up to the counseling area.

"Hey, Karen," the Christmas-caroling leader called out. "Come sing 'Jingle Bells' with us!"

I sang, I climbed up and down stairs, I made sure the shoppers were choosing quickly enough to keep the lines moving, I checked in with the counselors, made sure there was enough hot cocoa in the waiting area, enough free Bibles on the second floor, and figured out solutions for any problem that came about.

By the end of the day I was exhausted, but I felt amazing.

"You just helped bless a lot of families in this community today," Pastor Taylor said. "I knew you could do it. Way to go!"

Somehow he saw strength in me through the fragile brokenness. And, little by little, I began to see it, too.

PICTURES

As a Christmas gift for my mother, I made a book online of pictures from the last year. At this time, a year before, Gavin had made me a single mother. Dealing with the stress and depression that year felt enormous, but as I worked on this book I realized there had been so much more to the past year than I'd thought.

Pictures of us at the beach showed two happy little boys laughing in the waves, resting in my arms, rolling in soft sand. There was our trip to Vermont to visit my sister, where Tyler kissed a chicken on the beak at a nearby farm, milked a goat, and brushed the shiny brown fur of a beautiful cow. Upstate with my cousin, the boys rode their first kiddie roller coaster at a county fair. We swam with friends in Brooklyn and Long Island in the summer and enjoyed s'mores by a giant campfire with our new church family at a fall retreat. Brandon turned three and started preschool; Tyler turned two and was dedicated at church. When the book finally came in the mail, I turned its pages with incredible appreciation for the lesson in those pictures. Even in times of incredible heartache, there also lives incredible joy.

CHRISTMAS IN FLORIDA

Palm trees wrapped in Christmas lights, T-shirts in December, and sand under my feet instead of snow were just what I needed after working so hard the last few months. Adjusting to being a working, single mother was harder than I thought. If I thought keeping up with errands, housework, laundry, and food shopping was difficult before, it became even harder with a full-time job. I needed a rest, and Christmas in Florida with my family was just the place to do it.

Along with the whole New York crew, there were my mother's cousins, who lived near her, and my brother Jose, who lives three hours away from my parents.

We had just finished opening presents and it was time to sing. It was our tradition. Jose pulled out the guitar, and the family gathered around in the living room to sing "Silent Night," "Rudolph the Red-Nosed Reindeer," "Winter Wonderland," and Spanish Christmas songs called parranda music. Papi belted out the tenor part, my mother the soprano, and I took the alto, as usual. We all sang together, then debated which carol to sing next.

"'On the First Day of Christmas'!" my nephew yelled.

"No, that's always last!" my mother reminded. It was the grand finale, because it always cracked us up. Kevin's part was always "five golden rings," and he'd sing it in a mock opera voice, which always brought tears from laughing so hard.

"'O Holy Night,'" my father requested, and we all turned to the third page of our song sheets. We started together, but as Papi closed his eyes and raised his hand to his chest, we all quieted down to hear his beautiful tenor voice.

O night divine indeed.

BEDTIME STORY

Hey, Papi, why don't you tell the boys a bedtime story," I suggested.

I was trying to pack our bags for our trip to Disney the next day, but the boys were restless in their beds. "Tell them a story about when you were a little boy."

He shrugged his shoulders. "Okay," he said, then sat on the side of their bed, where they jumped around in breathless giggles.

"Come on, guys, control yourselves," he said in his heavy Spanish accent. The boys sat down but still wiggled around in excitement.

"Okay, your mother told me to tell you a story, so I'm going to tell you a story."

I chuckled as I packed the bags.

"When I was a little boy, like you two, I had no toys for Christmas. We were too poor. I had no shoes, I had no toothbrush—nothing! Sometimes we had no food. When I was ten years old, my father died. Dead!"

"The end," I interrupted, shaking my head, trying not to laugh.

"Gene," my mother said, catching the last part as she walked near the room. "What are you telling them that for?"

"Well, it's true," he said defensively.

I led my father out of the room with some good-try pats on the back and shut off the lights.

"Pleasant dreams, boys! Pleasant dreams."

THERE'S NO CRYING IN DISNEY WORLD

The Magic Kingdom with Kevin, his kids, and the boys was the perfect place to end the year 2011. Exactly a year before, I had been a weeping wreck. Now I was walking and dancing down Main Street toward Cinderella's Castle.

"Take a picture of me and the boys," I told Kevin, lifting both boys, one on each hip. They wanted to get down and started to fuss.

"Picture," I said, bouncing them up and down, trying to make them laugh. "Come on, smile."

"No!" Brandon shouted. "I don't want a picture!"

Both of them started to cry.

"Oh, come on," I said, spinning them around. "This is Disney! There's no crying in Disney World! It's a rule!"

I had done enough crying the past year for all of us combined, and now it was time to have some fun. They begged to differ.

"Oh, whatever—just take the picture," I said.

With happy music in the air and the castle as my backdrop, I held my grouchy boys and smiled the biggest smile I could—not just for the camera, but because I was happier than I'd ever imagined I could be.

WHAT I WAS DOING RIGHT

The moment I opened my eyes I was in a frenzy. I woke up late, had to pack overnight bags for the boys for their father, feed them, dress them, and run out the door in time for church—that was, of course, if Gavin wasn't late picking them up. I dug through the cart of clean clothes I hadn't had the energy to fold and put away the night before. Readjusting to work mode after such a great time in Florida was proving to be a challenge.

The boys woke up demanding oatmeal, then changed their minds once it was made. Tyler spilled his milk twice. Gavin was late, but it didn't even matter, because when he arrived I was still in pajamas running around like a crazy woman.

"Bye-bye, Mama," Tyler said.

"Bye, babies," I said, then pecked them quickly on their foreheads.

When they finally left I wanted to collapse back into my bed, but skipping out on church was not an option. Sunday was part of my workweek, and I had to do nursery. I'd forgotten to call other nursery workers to fill in the other slots, and I prayed someone would be available and willing. I ran out the door looking as tired and panicked as I felt and headed for the subway. As I boarded the first train, I realized I'd left my keys to the nursery at home. Now I had to figure out a way to get in! After my subway rides, I jogged the rest of the way to church. I huffed and puffed, wanting to have a tantrum like my kids, wanting to sleep, hating myself for always forgetting things, pitying my life as a single mother; every negative thought about my disappointments and failures wrapped around me until I could barely breathe. I arrived in the middle of praise and worship. Babies and toddlers go downstairs after the music, but so far I didn't see one child under four years old. I sat down, caught my breath, then quietly sang praises to God. I felt a little better. I kept looking at the back door, waiting for kids who never came. Pastor stepped up and, to my surprise, started to talk about me.

"We're just so grateful to Karen for all the great work she's doing with the children's ministry." He spoke about the events I'd organized, the after-school program during the week, and all my work with the kids on Sundays.

"She blesses so many children every day, and she is truly making an impact on each of their lives."

Everyone clapped and turned in their seats, smiling in my direction.

They didn't care what a wreck I was that morning, because, despite the craziness of my life, I was still doing what needed to be done. The lights dimmed and they put on a video I had made about our after-school kids. It had always made me smile and tear up as I watched their little faces and listened to the inspiring music. The tears came, but they were about more than just the video. I needed that encouragement more than ever that morning. I felt the personal care of God in that moment. He knew I needed to sit down, breathe, and get those negative thoughts out of my mind. I was focusing on all that was wrong in my life. But through Pastor Taylor's words, the video, the applause, and the encouraging smiles of the congregation, God reminded me what I was doing right.

HEALING

"Grieve. But let your grief be your process,
not your address."

BIKE

I bought my bike at a little sidewalk sale for fifty dollars. It was the first bike I had owned as an adult. I locked it up in the bike room of my apartment building and kept meaning to buy a helmet, but the busyness of life kept pushing it out of my mind. Then the cold weather came, and it stayed in that bike room for months. For a while, I even forgot I had one. When the spring came I finally bought a helmet and took my bike out of that dark little room. It was time.

Here we go, I thought as I got on and started pedaling down the street. There was a little fear, especially near the cars, but once I got to the bike path near the Hudson River I was zooming by and squealing like a little kid. The rush of life I felt in me was indescribable. I breathed in the smell of the water, watched the small boats sail by and the smiling people sprawled out on colorful picnic blankets on the grass. I stopped along the way to hear a street band and soak in the sun, but for the most part I just rode my bike all day. As I felt the sun and wind on my face, I thought of all those days I'd spent locked away in my own gloom, just like the bike in its dark little room. And now, after months of healing, it was this simple bike ride that completely freed me.

"Thank you for my life," I repeated over and over again. "Thank you, Lord, for my life!"

A few months later, my bike was stolen—it's New York City, after all. But I didn't wait long to get another one. There was nothing that could stop me from living now.

PAINTING HAPPINESS

There's something therapeutic about painting happiness on your walls. It's really amazing what a few gallons of butter-yellow paint can do to your soul. This was a new season for me, and I wanted my home to reflect not only my survival, but my hope and renewed joy.

I got rid of every painting and hung up blank white canvases, waiting for colors and inspiration. Old photos were taken down and new ones of the boys were framed. My dingy linoleum floors were now covered by bright laminate wood, and the dining room chairs were newly dressed in dark, childproof upholstery.

As my home was undergoing its slow rebirth, I asked advice from carpenters who had come to Graffiti on a missions trip from North Carolina. This was the team that cleaned, built, and repaired.

"I'm thinking of building a loft bed for my boys," I said, naively assuming I could do it myself.

Our only bedroom, with a twin and a full-size bed, wasn't spacious enough to store all their toys or move around in comfortably. I wanted their play area out of the living room and hoped a loft bed would transform their room into a space designed for years of fun and creativity.

"Why don't you wait till we get back to New York next month," the team suggested. "Then we can help you figure it out."

I was thrilled and agreed to wait.

In the meantime, I painted the boys' walls the color of sunny skies, and when the team finally returned, I was eager to get their input and go shopping for lumber.

"Hi," I shouted, greeting them with hugs.

They'd been working all day in the church and were having sandwiches in the basement.

"Got your bed all ready," the leader of the team, David, said.

"What?" I asked, not sure if I'd heard him right.

He pointed to a pile of lumber in a corner, some of the pieces already put together.

"Yup, got it all built. Just have to assemble it," he said in that North Carolina accent most of our teams spoke with—an accent I'd grown to identify as the sound of love.

"Oh," I said, caught a bit off guard. "How much do I owe for the wood?"

He shooed his hand as he took a bite of his sandwich.

"No, seriously, David," I pressed. "How much was it?"

"You don't owe anything. We raised the money for this."

The next day they came to the apartment to install the bed as the boys and I looked on excitedly.

"I do it!" Tyler squeaked.

David let Brandon and Tyler help, cupping their little hands on the drill or asking them to pass him screws and bolts. When it was done, Mike, Dave's assistant, hoisted the boys to the top.

The sun seemed to light up the room more brightly than ever as I watched my little ones touch the ceiling and squeal with joy.

I was overwhelmed by the generosity and kindness of this team, and I could feel God's hand in all of it. He'd done so much to transform me on the inside. And now he'd sent these incredible servants to help me transform everything else.

MOTHER'S DAY

W ake up, Princess," Brandon said, as I pretended to sleep.

"I'm waiting for a prince to kiss me," I whispered with a smirk, waiting for him to take the cue.

"Oh." He thought for a minute as I opened one eye. "Maybe Tyler can be the prince."

"Wow," I said, getting up and shaking my head with a laugh. "Thanks a lot, buddy. I feel the love."

I followed him into the kitchen, where he demanded cereal. Tyler shuffled to the table, his face still scrunched from just waking up.

"Hi, Mama," he said, climbing into the chair.

"Hi, baby," I said, getting a second bowl.

It was Mother's Day, my second one as a single mother, and I wasn't particularly looking forward to the day. At least those annoying Mother's Day commercials were finally going to come to an end.

"Happy Mother's Day, Mom!" the kids in the jewelry commercial would yell as they jumped into the giant, cozy white bed. The husband with the perfect teeth and jawline would lovingly place the breakfast tray before her, and by the end he would have placed a sparkling necklace around her neck.

There was no breakfast in bed for me, or flowers on the table that morning. No one would help my kids make cards with glue and glitter or whisk me away to a spa for a much-needed massage. How could I look forward to this day with no one to celebrate me?

"Cereal!"

I snapped out of my pity party and poured milk and Cheerios into their bowls. We had to get ready for church. At least there I would get the traditional rose and chocolate square.

I went into the room to figure out something to wear. Should I even bother getting dressed up?

Diane called as I was looking through the closet.

"Hey!" I said.

"Hi, what are you doing today?"

"Nothing. Just church."

"Okay, good. Kacy and I are coming over."

My mood brightened. I put on a pretty dress, went to church, got my rose and chocolate, came home, and changed into shorts and a tank top. Knowing restaurants would be packed and extra expensive, I defrosted a precooked lasagna. It was almost ready as Diane and her friend walked through the door.

"Titi Diane!" the boys screamed.

After they finished tackling her, I hugged her tight and breathed in her sweet-smelling perfume. *I should start wearing perfume,* I thought.

"So what do you want to do?" she asked.

I shrugged. What could we really do without reservations or a plan?

"Let's just eat now, and then have a picnic in the park," I suggested.

"Sounds good to me."

After lasagna, we walked to the park together.

We opened up the blanket where I normally held my music classes, between the two large oak trees. I set out fruit, Goldfish crackers, and chips. The boys played with a ball and we girls played a board game. I won.

In the following hours, we played with the boys, rested in the sun, and made each other laugh.

"Thank you for coming today," I said to Diane. "It turned out to be a perfect day." I was happy to be out and enjoying the wonderful weather. But as I watched the other families nearby, complete with kids, Mom, and Dad, I realized I had used the wrong word. I had finally let go of Gavin, but I was having a harder time letting go of my family. Yes, it was a nice day, but it wasn't perfect. Mother's Day would never be perfect for me.

JUST LIKE YOU CHANGE YOUR COAT

I sat in Pastor Taylor's office going over the logistics for the week, and before we closed out in prayer I shared with him my Mother's Day realization.

"Do you know what Vaughn used to say?" Pastor Taylor asked, referring to a dear member of our church who'd passed away recently. Vaughn had been homeless for years and had lived a difficult life, but in our church he became a beloved elder and friend. "This was what he'd say to people who were having a hard time letting go of their woes: 'Everything you're telling me might be true. Yes, your circumstances might be hard, what someone did to you might be really unfair, and I bet that person really did hurt you. But if you keep focusing on it, it will kill you.' That's what he used to say, Karen, and I'm telling you that if you want to heal, you have to stop focusing on all the negative things in your life. You can grieve, but let it be your process, not your address."

"But how," I asked, wiping my tears, feeling annoyed that I was always wiping tears. "If that's how I feel every time I see a family, how can I change what I feel?"

Pastor Taylor leaned forward in his chair and looked right at me.

"Focus on what you have. You can change your attitude like you change your coat. It's a choice. You don't have to wear it. You can choose to take it off and wear something else—focus on something else. Don't keep thinking about what you can't do, think about what you can do; don't keep your focus on what you don't have, focus on what you do have and what you can give. Don't focus on what you feel Gavin did to you, focus on forgiveness."

I nodded. It made sense. He handed me a tissue.

"And you can do it," he added. "You know why?"

I blew my nose and chuckled. I knew the answer he was looking for.

"Because I'm Karen Valentin."

CAMPING TRIP

Where are you guys going?" our doorman asked as we stepped out of the elevator. Two rolled-up sleeping bags rested on the awning of the stroller, Brandon and Tyler each carried a superhero backpack stuffed more than usual, and my giant backpack looked like a boulder.

"Camping," I said, giving him a look that screamed *Yikes!*

His eyes widened and he shook his head.

"Wow! You are a brave woman." He laughed. "Good luck!"

I knew what he really meant was "You're crazy," and I would definitely need more than just luck. I had to schlep all of this stuff on the subway with a two-year-old and a four-year-old, then keep them entertained for two hours on a bus heading to the New Jersey Crawfish Music Festival.

At least I didn't have to bring the tents, I thought, trying to make myself feel better as I began the adventure toward the subway. My friend Laura, who had invited us, would bring those.

I knew the doorman was right. I was crazy even to try; but mostly I was excited for the boys to have this new experience.

We arrived exhausted, but once the tent was up, the boys had fun going in and out of our little nylon shelter. The porta-potties were a nightmare, but the boys got to pluck a banjo brought by one of our tent neighbors, who was happy to see them light up over the instrument.

"Let's go over to the music pavilion," Laura said.

They had set up colorful blankets on the grass, one filled with toys, and had even brought a small baby pool for the kids to splash around in. We ate crawfish and other yummy food as we listened to live jazz music. It suddenly felt great to be "crazy" and bring my kids to a place like this. I knew Irma would be proud.

That night we toasted marshmallows and the boys made s'mores for the first time.

Laura set out a spread of food outside the tents that was amazing.

"I want peanut-butter-and-jelly," Brandon whined.

"There's no peanut-butter-and-jelly, but there's all this other delicious stuff here you can try."

"I want peanut-butter-and-*jelly!*" he screamed, then started to cry.

"Well, Brandon," I said, "you can choose to be upset about something you don't have, or you can come over here and enjoy all this yummy food that's right here. It's really up to you." Suddenly Pastor Taylor's words clicked more than ever before. Brandon wiped his tears and walked over to look at the other wonderful choices.

After dinner, we strolled over to a smaller music showcase, and my silly, dancing boys with their inflatable guitars got an invitation to join the musicians onstage.

I filled my camera with all the incredible moments and memories we made during those two short days camping out with our friends. It was worth the trip to get there, the stinky porta-potties, the uncomfortable, cramped night in our tent. Despite the discomfort and inconvenience, I knew I'd continue to be "crazy" and make the most of this wonderful life. I would focus on creating new and exciting experiences for myself and for these beautiful kids I'd been given.

TO TAKE A BREATH

After a hectic few days of nonstop busyness, I readied myself for a treat on my to-do list: a trip to the hair salon. I arrived more than an hour early. This rare instance of having nothing else to do gave me permission to take a breath, slow down, and just relax. I strolled into an Indian shop, shelves piled high with spices colored in gorgeous reds and earth tones. The Indian music and pungent scent of the store transported me to another world. Next door to the Indian store was a new dessert shop, where the ice cream was handmade. Farther down I discovered a vintage candy store where childhood memories were sold with the tasty sweets. I bought a sandwich at the corner deli and had a quiet picnic on mosaic steps across the street from the salon. The tulips were in full bloom, and the trees were dressed in flowers as well. With each gentle breeze, tiny white petals fell like confetti over me. I felt so blessed to live life in that beautiful moment without the distraction of being busy. It was a wonderful reminder to breathe in life like that more often.

DRIVER'S LICENSE

"Okay, so now your seat belt is on. What do you do next?" my co-worker Kareem asked as I sat in the driver's seat of his car.

"Adjust the mirrors," I said confidently.

"Very good."

I'd made the decision finally to go for my driver's license. While unnecessary in the city, I wanted the freedom to take my boys anywhere. If the boys wanted to see cows, I wanted to show them cows; if they wanted to eat real ice cream—instead of my sister's "healthy" version while visiting her Upstate—I wanted to get in a car and take them for ice cream.

After several lessons circling the Lower East Side, I was finally ready to take my road test.

"Good luck," Diane said as she stepped out of the car.

I held the steering wheel, breathing as if I were feeling a contraction. "Thanks."

The lady giving me the road test sat in the passenger seat without responding to my hello.

She wrote some notes, then said, "Pull out."

I readjusted the mirrors, which were already adjusted, put on my belt, and switched the gear to drive.

I approached a stop sign and did just as Kareem and Diane had taught me. Stop, look, and roll gently forward.

"Let's go," she barked in a heavy Brooklyn accent. "What are you waiting for?"

"Sorry," I practically whispered, squeezing the steering wheel tighter than I already was.

I made a broken U-turn, went around the block, signaled, and turned my head before passing.

"Park here," she said.

I did. Perfectly.

"Pull out again and make a left."

I made a right.

"I said make a left!" she screamed, her accent getting thicker. "What is wrong with you? We were done!"

I shrank in the driver's seat. I didn't respond.

"Pull over there."

I did.

She sat there in silence, writing on the form in her clipboard.

Diane walked over to the car and looked at me through the windshield. I peeked at her and shook my head. I knew I'd failed.

"You passed," the lady said bluntly, handing me a piece of paper. "Here."

My eyes opened in shock as she walked out without another word. Diane stepped in, and the two of us screamed in celebration as I told her "I did it!"

POOL

After eleven months of being a working mom, I could now enjoy a whole month off with my boys in Florida. This time I could pay for our own tickets.

Now a licensed driver, I didn't have to be chauffeured by my parents. I took the boys to the playground by myself, drove to Walmart to pick up new swimming trunks for Brandon and Tyler, and even ventured to the beach alone. I didn't have to drop the boys off at day care, squeeze into a crowded train, walk up and down stairs, work for eight hours, and take the trains back home again. I could relax. The boys and I could spend time together playing in the pool instead of them being cooped up in day care. I was with my mother and father, I was driving everywhere, and I wanted this feeling to last forever.

I signed up the boys for gymnastics camp near my parents' house. The price was reasonable, I knew the boys would have a blast, and it would give me four whole hours of lazy suntanning time without them!

⌒

I sat with my mother near the swimming pool munching on the grapes she'd packed for us. We sat there lazily talking for a while, then I dipped in the water to cool off. I spun around with my arms wide and swam backwards, looking at the blue sky above. I dove under and held my breath to see how far I could go before coming up for air. My mother sat there in her big sun hat watching me, smiling. I did handstands near her, pointing my toes like I learned from years of gymnastics, then rose to the surface to look at my mother once again. I felt like a nine-year-old little girl as my mother smiled at me from under her hat while I did "Watch me" tricks in the water. I treasured that small moment in time with her, and enjoyed the most carefree hours I'd felt in years.

WELCOME HOME

We're home," I said, exhausted from the flight, walking through our apartment door. Brandon and Tyler went right to their toys. They were happy to be back. I needed more convincing. I felt claustrophobic in the small apartment—big for Manhattan, small for Florida. I'd have to return to work in a few days and get the boys back to day care. I wasn't looking forward to the trains, and I didn't know when I would drive a car again. Going back to single, working-mom life in New York City would take some adjusting to—again.

I walked into the bathroom to wash away the travel grime and this negative attitude that was steadily growing. When I pulled back the shower curtain, a giant water bug greeted me.

"Welcome home," I said under my breath, looking for a shoe to kill it. "Welcome home."

MOVIE NIGHT

It was Monday, movie night at our place. We opened up the sofa in front of the television, snuggled under blankets in our pajamas, and ate buttery microwaved popcorn. That evening, instead of our usual cartoon movie pick, I decided to show the boys something different. As a Christmas gift years ago, I had made my family a DVD of all our old home movies. I thought the boys would get a kick out of seeing old footage of the family.

"Look, guys," I said, pointing to me as a little girl. "There I am when I was Tyler's age!" Tyler was completely amused and giggled under the covers. A different clip came up, one of me when I was an infant. My mother cradled a very upset baby Karen, then placed me in my carriage. "That's me when I was a baby," I said with a laugh.

"Who was taking care of us when you were a baby?" Brandon demanded to know.

"Oh," I said, "you weren't here yet." He looked confused. I tried again. "You weren't born yet when Mami was a baby. I had to grow up before you could be born." Brandon's big brown eyes welled up in tears. "This is scary!" he cried. I tried to comfort him by explaining it better, but that just freaked him out even more. I took out the home movie and quickly put in a Disney movie instead.

HURRICANE SANDY

It was two days after Hurricane Sandy, the storm that flooded and devastated much of the East Coast. The Upper West Side of Manhattan, where I live, was unaffected. Downtown, Graffiti didn't get off as easy. I wanted to help, and since there was virtually no public transportation, I had to Rollerblade over a hundred blocks to get there. I skated through a fully functional uptown, with undamaged shops opened for business. But as I continued downtown I encountered another world. The traffic lights were darkened as far as I could see. The stores were all closed; there was not even an open deli where I could buy a bottle of water. After all that Rollerblading, I regretted not carrying a bottle with me. Everywhere I looked I saw damage from the storm: signs were torn down, trees rested on the streets, and damaged items from flooded apartments lined the sidewalks—furniture, toys, clothing, and appliances. People looked tired and defeated. I arrived to a similar scene at the church. A growing pile of our things, now garbage, filled the sidewalk. But one thing was different: there wasn't a look of defeat on those who busied themselves with the cleanup. I, too, felt positive in the midst of our loss. As sad as I was to see our things gone (especially our after-school supplies), I was more overwhelmed by the flood of volunteers that showed up. Many wonderful teams drove up with truckloads of water, flashlights, snacks, a generator, and a pump to empty the water from our basement. In no time, the floors were dry. They were our heroes, but it didn't stop there. Throughout the next few weeks, more teams came to help our neighbors dry out and prevent mold. A new ministry was born in our church to help hurricane victims replace lost items and receive counseling. Hundreds donated money and new items for our children's ministry, and our other ministries as well.

Through all this, I thought about the song I used to play over and over, "I'll Praise You in This Storm." The out-of-state teams, our church, and those who loved us weren't just praising him through the storm; they were spreading the love and hope of Jesus in the midst of it. I knew that was the person I wanted to become. Not just the woman who survived, but the one who gave hope and love to others going through the same storm.

NEW YEAR'S EVE

It was a few days before the New Year, and my parents were still in town for the holidays.

"I think I'm going to do something fun this year," I told my mother, "maybe something even glamorous."

It had been a long time since I had enjoyed my New Year's Eve, and the last few I'd wished I were anywhere but home watching television while the boys slept.

While I initially envisioned something fancy, it was clear I wasn't going to wear a ball gown to a fancy gala, but I did have a few options: a small gathering at a friend's house, Times Square with some coworkers, or a bigger party downtown as a friend's guest.

By the day of, I decided on the small gathering at my friend's house. It sounded perfect and like less of a hassle than the other two choices.

~~

"Good night," I said with kisses after I read to the boys. It was time to get ready and make myself pretty.

"What are you going to wear?" my mother asked, snuggled under blankets on the couch. The pre-countdown entertainment had begun, and my mother switched between channels to see it all.

"I don't know," I said lazily, snuggling in with her.

"Karen, you want ice cream?" My father asked from the kitchen.

"Ooo, yeah!" I shouted.

"Me, too!" my mother echoed.

The boys were chatting and making noise in their room. I didn't want to get up to shush them; I was too comfy.

"Guys!" I yelled, banging on the wall. "Quiet down and go to sleep."

My father delivered two large bowls of chocolate ice cream, and we watched footage of New Year's celebrations in Australia and Europe, where it had already struck midnight.

"Awww, Paris," I said excitedly, watching the colorful fireworks spray out over the Eiffel Tower.

By ten thirty it was clear I didn't want to go anywhere. I called my friend and told her I was staying home with my family. The year before, I had been aching to go somewhere exciting. I'd felt trapped. But this time I felt completely content to be with my parents, whom I don't often see, and listening to my kids, who were still chatting away in their room. It wasn't the most exciting New Year's Eve, but I was exactly where I wanted to be.

SATURDAYS

More than ever, Saturdays were my favorite day of the week. I didn't have to shake sleepy boys out of their dreams, speed through the morning with quick bowls of cereal, search for missing shoes, or panic when it started to get late. Saturdays were the only time I could wake up when I wanted and let the boys sleep in.

"Mami," Tyler called from his room.

I peeked in the door.

"Snuggle," he said, smiling.

I scooped him into my arms under the covers and kissed his warm, chubby cheeks.

"Mama," Brandon said, looking down from the loft bed, then climbing down to snuggle, too. I kissed him until he giggled, and then he sighed. "You love me." I melted over his words.

Feeling the love, I was inspired to sing sweetly, because I was feeling like Snow White with her little dwarfs.

"You are my sunshine, my only sunshine," I sang.

Then, ever so gently, Brandon put his little hand over my mouth. I got the hint and stopped.

"I'm going to tell you a story, Mami," Tyler said, then started talking in gibberish.

"Aw, come on. Tell me a real story," I protested.

"That *is* a real story," he insisted.

"Oh yeah? In what language?"

"In Funny!"

Touché, little man.

We shuffled to the kitchen, where I had the round glass table all set, including fresh flowers that I'd bought yesterday. Surrounding the flowers was a spread of bagels, yogurt, fresh strawberries, and home-made oatmeal. I'd spent the day before giving the apartment a good cleaning and had shopped for all my breakfast goodies. The sun was pouring in from the large kitchen window, making the apartment look even brighter and cleaner.

We sat there together, munching on our breakfast and listening to music.

"Oh, I love this song!" I said. The boys laughed as I sang into the spoon.

The next one was a salsa song, and I jumped up out of my chair and danced around the table. The boys followed me. We spun around and wiggled our hips in our pajamas. It was glorious, as most Saturdays were. There was nothing pressing to do, nowhere we needed to go—just the business of enjoying life and each other.

HIS AND HERS

Gavin and I sat at the large wooden table with two copies of our divorce papers in neat white piles, his and hers. I felt strong. I wasn't as fragile as the last few times we'd almost signed. It had taken us awhile to set up mediation and draft our separation agreement. Then, for months after that, there was always some-thing that caused a delay in the final signing—missing information, something we'd forgotten to bring, a canceled ap-pointment by Gavin. Each time I wondered, *Lord, is this you? Are you going to turn things around?*

The mediator smiled sympathetically as we took our seats. "Shall we go over the document to make sure everything is in order?"

I knew there would be no restoration. God didn't turn things around. There would be no more delays. The strength I felt that morning slowly faded as I held the pen in my hand and signed my name.

I walked to the station, and on a crowded train back home I had to disappear into my jacket to muffle my sobs.

"Why didn't you intervene?" my heart quietly asked. "Why couldn't you make us a family?" After all that time of healing and acceptance I now had to mourn all over again.

I got home and opened the door. The boys ran to me as usual. Their sweet, happy faces urged me not to forever dwell on what I'd lost. So I hugged them tightly, holding on to what I still had, holding on to what was yet to come.

ACCORDION

"Good night," I said as I left work. It had been a long day, my body was tired, and the thought of having to walk over ten blocks to the subway was torture. I dragged myself along as I thought about my day and everything I still had to do. It made me want to stop right there and go to sleep on a park bench. For weeks, my days had played out exactly like this one. I'd rush in the morning to get the boys ready for school, negotiating what they'd eat, what they'd wear, who'd press the elevator button. After a train and bus to work, I'd sometimes be too busy even to stop for lunch. Back at home, Brandon and Tyler would run around like two little tornadoes as I'd try to fix dinner, do laundry, straighten up, wash dishes, and, finally, get them ready for bed.

As I entered the subway, I wondered if my life was always going to be this hectic and tiring. I wished I could enjoy life and my kids instead of feeling like I just had to get through each day. I slumped onto a bench, waiting for my train, as an older gentleman began playing his accordion. The music instantly brought my mind back to the time when I'd lived in France. My body relaxed, and the heaviness seemed to lift off my eyes, my shoulders, and my heart. The train station no longer seemed so glum. I thought of snowcapped mountains, Paris at night, and all the wonderful people I'd met during my stay. There had been such adventure, wonder, and discovery in my life, and, as he played, I felt a sense of hope. The memories of living in France reminded me that life wasn't always a struggle. And, as the music played, I became convinced that it wouldn't always be.

DIVORCE PARTY

I gripped the trapeze bar with my hands as I stood on the edge of the platform forty feet above the net. Diane, my sister-in-law, and seven other close girlfriends of mine watched as I got ready to fly through the air with the greatest of ease.

This was my divorce party. Someone had suggested I have one to celebrate my freedom, but that hadn't seemed like something to celebrate. I didn't want my freedom. I hadn't signed up for that when I had gotten married. When I'd said "I do," it had been because I wanted to be joined with my husband and do life together, side by side. I wanted us both to raise our children and grow old with each other, like my parents, who'd been married over forty years.

"Okay, maybe you don't want to celebrate your freedom," she had said. "But there's still a lot to celebrate." The more she spoke, the more I agreed I should have a party. I had booked the trapeze school and invited the women who had rallied around me through the last few years.

"Are you ready to jump?"asked the instructor, who stood with me on the platform.

"Yes," I said.

I held on with all my might, and glided through the air as the girls cheered me on, celebrating my survival, my newfound strength, my courage, and my excitement for new adventures.

CHILD SUPPORT

Gavin hadn't given us money in over a year. Having lived with him, I knew he wasn't good at managing money. As long as he was taking the boys regularly and picking them up from day care when I worked late on Wednesdays, I didn't push it. Every time we discussed money it ended in tension, and I just didn't want to deal with it.

He'd recently moved to New Jersey, and I wondered if that would affect our schedule with the boys. It did.

I can't pick up the boys on Wednesdays anymore, he'd texted me.

Great! Now I'd have to pay a babysitter for four hours a week while I worked late, on top of all the other bills I was paying.

"Why don't you just take him to court?" my friends would ask. "Then you don't have to bring up money with him ever again. The court will handle it."

I had always said no. I didn't want to create a bigger divide. But now I was upset. All he had to do was take care of himself. Unlike me, he was free to work as many hours as he chose without worrying about child care, and yet he still couldn't help us financially. I'd given him enough time. No matter how much I asked, or argued, I knew this would always be an issue.

~~

I paced the courtroom lobby, dressed like a businesswoman. *Maybe I should have worn something more casual,* I thought, looking at the others.

The elevator doors opened and Gavin walked out. We saw each other but didn't even nod hello. Moments later they called our names, and we walked down the long corridor together in silence. I could feel my insides slowly tie up in knots.

We walked inside, and it looked intimidatingly official. Even the signing of our divorce papers had taken place in a small room with a large table. Other than being a juror, this was my first time in a courtroom.

The magistrate walked in.

"You may be seated."

We sat down.

She addressed me first, and I nervously spoke, handing a security guard all of my paperwork.

He owed thousands of dollars.

"What do you have to say for yourself, sir?" the magistrate asked.

She let him speak. I don't remember much of what he said in his defense, but the words she spoke after he was done I will never forget.

~~

"Ms. Valentin. Are you seeking incarceration at this time?"

I was shocked. Apparently, even I hadn't fully understood the severity of Gavin abandoning his responsibilities. I looked over at him; he looked shocked, too.

"No ma'am," I said.

⌒

We walked back down the corridor in silence again.

"It's over," he finally said as we waited for the elevator.

"What's over?"

"It's over. I'm done. I'm out of your life for good."

"I know you're out of my life," I said. "You've been out of my life for a long time, and I'm okay with that. Are you talking about the boys?"

Silence.

"What do I tell the boys?" I asked.

Silence in the elevator, silence in the main entrance lobby, silence as we walked out the door.

"What do I tell the boys!" I said louder.

He unlocked the chain to his bicycle, which was tied to a lamppost.

"What do I tell the *boys!*" I screamed.

He got on his bike and, just before he rode off, he looked at me and spewed, "Tell them it's your fault they don't have a father."

FATHER'S DAY

After court, I picked up the boys from day care. It was Friday, and Father's Day was coming up in two days. I just knew what was coming as I walked through the door.

"Mami," they yelled, running to show me their handmade cards. Brandon's was in the shape of a dinosaur with wooden triangles glued to the creature's back. Tyler's had a picture of himself on the front, and inside a quote from Tyler written by his teacher: "I want to be like you when I grow up." I ached for them as they showed me each one with pride.

"We have to give these to Daddy for Father's Day," Brandon said in his raspy little voice.

The next day, to my relief, Gavin left a text message on my phone. *Have the boys ready by 1pm.*

The boys delivered their cards and spent Father's Day with their dad. But after he dropped them off and said good-bye, the boys wouldn't see him again for more than a year.

GRANDMA EVELYN

Grandma!" Brandon shouted, running into my mother-in-law's arms.

"Bran Bran!" she shouted, lifting him up.

"Where's Tyler?" I said dramatically, pointing to his hiding spot. "I don't know where he went!"

"Oh, no, where's my Ty Ty," she said, creeping over to the closet. His little giggles echoed from behind the door. "Tyler! Oh, I'm so sad. Where could my baby be?"

Tyler burst through the closet: "Boo, Grandma!"

"Ty Ty!"

She held him tight and spun around.

"You happy, baby?" I asked when she put him down and he started dancing around her.

"No," he said. "I dancin.'"

Evelyn, who'd been a wonderful grandmother from the beginning, stepped up even more after Gavin wasn't present. She'd take them for the weekend at least once a month to give me rest, she'd spoil them with toys and new clothes, and she always encouraged me as their mother.

"You're doing a great job!" she'd always say. "You're a great mother!"

In the midst of our divorce, she told me, with tears in her eyes, "Karen, I just want you to know that even though my son can't see it, he married a treasure of a wife. He may not be able to see it, but I do."

Evelyn, Gavin's sisters, and their daughters—whom I never stopped calling my nieces—were family, and an important part of our life. We spent Mother's Day and other holidays together, and took the kids to fun places like Sesame Place. Evelyn prayed for us daily, trusting that God had a plan for our lives and that Gavin would step back into his role as father.

I prayed for the same things, and thanked him with all my heart for Gavin's family, who never left our side.

THE MOUNTAIN

I spent four weeks in July consumed in our Graffiti summer program. Kids enjoyed fine art, sports, and performing arts in the morning, then water balloon fights and sprinklers after lunch. I wondered if the boys were having as much fun in day care as the Graffiti kids were. I knew they weren't.

When July was over, I had the whole month of August off, and I couldn't wait to make it up to the boys.

I got my very first rental car Upstate and planned out the whole week at our very own summer home—my sister's house.

"You might want to read what's in that stuff," Diane said as I stocked up with food I knew the boys liked.

I looked for the nutrition facts on the box of cookies I'd just picked up.

"Let's see. It has one hundred percent of deliciousness." I put it in the cart. "Perfect."

My sister's all-natural choices didn't cut it for the boys or myself.

With the fridge filled with artificial flavors and plenty of gas in the car, we were set for an awesome week.

We went to a horse farm. The boys learned how to groom them and feed them peppermints. We had lazy days on the lake, picked berries in the orchards, and had evening barbecues on the porch with Diane.

I bit into a buttery corn on the cob and talked about my plans for the next day. I wanted to take the boys hiking up Mount Beacon.

"What are you, nuts?" she said. "That's a difficult hike. I went with the girls last year, and everyone kept stopping and lying on the ground. It was ridiculous."

"I think we can do it!" I said, not ready to change my plans.

"You're going to climb a mountain with a three- and five-year-old?" she said, shaking her head with a laugh. "Good luck with all that!"

The next morning I drove to the starting point. I put on my big knapsack filled with water bottles and snacks for the trail.

"You ready, guys?" I asked.

"Yeah!" they shouted.

The boys walked ahead of me and found walking sticks taller than they were. Brandon was running, hopping, and doing ninja moves up the hill. Tyler tried to catch up, doing a few silly moves himself. I was already huffing and puffing and began to think, *Maybe this really was a crazy idea.*

The boys kept me going, as they had always done. I helped them up some steep areas, took breaks to rest and eat, and just kept going when Tyler started to complain and when it felt like it would never end. Then, almost like it had sneaked up on us, we had reached the top.

"We did it!" I shouted, looking out at the incredible view of where we had come from. "We did it, guys!"

The boys lifted their walking sticks as I snapped their picture. Brandon took a picture of me holding up my fingers in a peace sign. I welled up with emotion and pride at what we had done together. These were my boys. We were a team. And together we could accomplish anything.

THE CAR

Close to the end of the week, I was driving like a pro. I didn't want to give up my little car that took us to so many fun places.

"Come on, guy!" I yelled behind closed windows. "Let's move it." These slow drivers were a pain. I passed him on my right and continued driving in that lane. My favorite song that summer came on the radio and I turned up the volume, singing at the top of my lungs. I was enjoying my car, loving the country life, and oblivious to the fact that I was in the wrong lane.

I drove into a curve going about sixty miles an hour, and as the road straightened out I saw a red car coming straight toward us. I swerved to the other lane just in time.

"Oh, my God. Oh, my God," I kept repeating. I felt my body shaking the rest of the way to Diane's house. The boys were fast asleep in the back, oblivious to the fact that I'd almost killed us all.

DADDY LOVES YOU

I was making breakfast when I heard Tyler whimpering in his bed. I opened the door and wrapped him in my arms.

"What's the matter, honey?" I asked, kissing his curls.

"I had a dream that Daddy died."

"Oh, no! That's scary, I know, but it's just a dream. Daddy's okay."

"How do you know?"

"I just do."

"Can we call him?"

"Sorry, baby, we can't. I don't have his number."

"I want to talk to Daddy," he pleaded.

Brandon woke up too and snuggled in with us.

"We haven't seen Daddy in a long time. Why can't we see him?"

I didn't know how to answer this. What could I say to them that wouldn't make them feel unwanted? How could I explain something even I couldn't understand? My anger for Gavin stirred as I watched my kids mourn their father when they didn't have to. How could he just disappear? How could he do this to them?

"I don't know," I finally said. "But I do know that you will see him again. And when you do, you can ask him that question."

"Daddy loves you both very much," I added, even though I now had a hard time believing it myself.

SPOONFUL OF HONEY

My boys played in the living room as I coughed in bed. I lay there, useless, crumpled-up tissues scattered on the blanket, the humidifier spewing its steady stream of cool mist, and the smell of Vicks VapoRub hanging in the air. I wanted a nice warm cup of soothing tea but didn't have the energy to get up and make it. I retreated into my quilt, feeling a slight pang of single-mom self-pity. *Nobody takes care of me,* I thought.

I ached for someone to fuss over me and make me feel better. Someone to make me a cup of chamomile like my father used to do, or a concoction of lemon juice with honey like my mother always made. There was no hand to touch my forehead and check for fever; no one to say a small prayer like I did for my children. As my sad little pity-party thoughts swirled around, I could hear the boys clanking around in the kitchen. What mess were they getting into now? I wondered miserably.

"Boys, what are you doing?" I attempted to yell through my sore throat.

No response.

I should go and see what's happening, I thought. But my aching body chose to ignore it.

Tyler peeked his head through the door.

"Mami, close your eyes and count to six," he said.

I grunted in protest, but I shut my eyes and counted.

When I opened them, Brandon held out a big silver spoon overflowing with honey.

"Surprise," he said proudly, "to make you better."

It was the sweetest spoonful of honey I have ever had.

THE MOTHER GOD MADE ME TO BE

"He will shelter you with his wings."

FAMILY PHOTO

Moms I knew said these three words without a second thought: *in our family*. We're big fans of Indian food in our family. In our family, we all have allergies. In our family, we love to get out in the country as much as we can. In our family this, and in our family that. I could never say those words without feeling strange.

"Me and the boys"—that was what I'd say: "Me and the boys are addicted to ice cream." Because that's what it was, just me—and the boys.

"But, Karen, of course you're a family," my sister argued when we spoke about my reluctance to say it.

"Yes, I know we are, technically," I tried to clarify. "But it just doesn't feel like a complete family. I don't feel comfortable saying it." I knew what I was saying didn't really make sense. But I had a vision of what family was. The boys and I had a missing piece, and without the presence of a husband and father I just couldn't say *in our family*.

Months after the conversation with my sister, I "liked" and shared a photography Facebook page to support the husband of a friend's new business. The gesture entered me in a contest that I didn't think twice about actually winning. I won.

⌒

The day of our free photo shoot, we dressed in jeans and white dress shirts. Gerson, the photographer, advised us to look like a unit after we'd discussed what I wanted from the photo shoot. I had told him about my complicated relationship with the word *family*, and I hoped the pictures would help me embrace us as one.

Gerson snapped pictures of us at home playing in the boys' room and snuggling on the couch. We went outside, and he took pictures of us by their favorite climbing tree in Central Park, strolling the sidewalk holding hands, and me smiling as they let go and ran ahead of me.

Days later he sent the images to me over the Internet. They were absolutely beautiful. I shared them on my Facebook page, and the responses came flooding in. "What a beautiful family," people said over and over again. As I framed my favorite family photo and hung it on the living room wall, I couldn't agree more.

INSOMNIAC CHILD

H ere, Mami," Tyler says, handing me a Band-Aid. "For your boo-boos. If you have a boo-boo."

I take the Band-Aid without a word and direct him back to his room with my squinting eyes. He smiles, flashing his dimples, and slowly disappears into the bedroom.

Moments later he reappears.

"Mami, when I wake up, give me a piece of paper because I know how to make a fan."

He runs back to his bed.

I know I should give him a stern warning, but this is entertaining now, and I wait to see what else he'll do.

"Look, Ma, I can whistle!" He sings a high-pitched note. It makes me cover my ears. It's not a whistle.

Disappears and reappears.

"Look, Ma!" He's put his arms through the neck hole of his shirt and is now wearing it as a tube top. "I put on my shirt." He does the chicken dance back to the room.

He's gone for a while. Perhaps the show is over. Nope, I'm wrong.

"*Uno, dos, tres, quarto, cinco*. Ta-da! I counted in Spanish."

When he comes back out I finally pick him up and lie with him until my insomniac child falls asleep, snoring like an overweight middle-aged man.

I know I'm doing it all wrong. It's not what the books say to do or how "Supernanny" does it on TV. But by the time bedtime comes, I'm too tired to fight another battle with the boys. I lie there thinking about all the other things I'm doing wrong as a mom: the sweets I'd give them, the hours of cartoons whenever I needed them quiet and hypnotized, the lack of green vegetables, the yelling instead of a calm, stern voice, the inconsistency in my rules and discipline. *I'm not really good at this,* the perfectionist in me thinks, *I need to do better.* But the other part of me comes to my own defense, the part of me that understands how overwhelmed I feel at times, the part of me who knows how much I love my kids despite it all. Before I close my eyes and fall asleep next to my son, that part of me whispers, "You're doing the best you can."

SANTA

Brandon opened the little wrapped shoebox that was handed to him by a white-bearded man. He wasn't playing Santa Claus. His name was Rusty, and he was part of a team from North Carolina who'd visited our New York City church to give early Christmas surprises to the children in our ministry. Brandon was delighted with each simple gift. "ChapStick!" he screamed. "Crayons! Toothpaste!" His favorite item was the little black yo-yo. He ran to the man with the friendly bearded face to show him what he'd received. The two of them spent a bit of time playing with the yo-yo.

"Okay, so you have to let it go, and just as it gets to the bottom, you lift your hand up again," Rusty explained.

Brandon looked carefully at each demonstration.

"I got it!" he cheered when he finally got the hang of it. I was grateful for the fatherly attention Brandon was receiving. It had been six months now since his own father had chosen to no longer be in his life.

Awhile later, I heard Brandon crying.

"What's wrong?" I asked him, cupping his cheeks in my hands.

"My yo-yo broke!" he cried.

"Okay, baby. Well, let me see it. Maybe I can fix it."

He pointed over at Rusty, who was already trying hard to put the yo-yo back together.

When it became obvious it couldn't be fixed, Brandon cried even harder.

Eventually he calmed down as we handed out the Christmas cupcakes. Brandon bit through the sprinkled frosting and smiled with vanilla cream on his lips. The yo-yo was long forgotten. But as I looked for Rusty to thank him for trying to fix it, I couldn't find him.

"Where did he go?" I asked one of the other team members.

"Oh, he went to Kmart to buy another yo-yo for Brandon," she said.

"What?" I shrieked. "That's over ten blocks away!" Outside it was snowing and the temperature had dropped to freezing. I was shocked.

But, more than that, I was touched that this man went out of his way in the snow for my son. When he came back bundled up against the cold, holding the small bag, I knew this was better than any mythical Santa Claus. This precious servant, who had so much God-given love in his heart, gave Brandon so much more than just a yo-yo that day. He showed my little boy, the kid with an absent father, that he was worth the trouble of a long winter walk and deserving of such sacrificial love.

HE'S MISSING ALL OF THIS

It was another beautiful day in Florida, and the ocean water was perfect. I went ahead of the boys and watched them squeal in delight with each wave that crashed into their suntanned bellies. I scooped them both up, planting kisses all over their wet faces.

"Mami, let's jump the waves together!" they said excitedly. We stood side by side and counted as each wave approached.

"One, two, three," we all cried, then jumped together, laughing each time. I swam backwards toward the deep water, looking up at the bright sky scattered with thin, wispy clouds. I looked back toward my boys and just smiled at the sheer joy in their faces.

He's missing all of this, I thought, not with anger, or sadness for my boys. This time, it was for Gavin . He didn't get to enjoy this moment like I did. He wasn't there at Disney World the day before, as the lights from the electrical parade projected colors onto their wonder-filled faces. For a year now, he hadn't gotten to hear their giggles as they played with each other or seen the pride in their eyes when they learned to swim. Anger, pride—whatever the excuse could possibly be, he was allowing it to steal away these moments with Brandon and Tyler, moments he could never get back. For the first time in a long time, we were not the victims of the choices he had made. He was.

I WAS SAD WHEN YOU SANG

It was Good Friday, and I was asked to sing "Via Dolorosa" at my old church. It was great to see all the people I missed and loved. I wasn't able to visit on Sundays, but singing "Via Dolorosa" on Good Friday was turning into a tradition.

"Karen, you're singing today?" Mrs. Singleton asked, excited.

"Yes," I said, just as excited, giving her a big hug hello.

The boys sat in the front with a friend as I took my place at the microphone. The somber music began, and I sang about the long walk Jesus made to Calvary.

"Mami, I was sad when you sang," Brandon said after the service.

"Why, baby?" I asked.

"Remember when you cried at my graduation in preschool?" he said.

"Yes."

"You said you were crying because you were proud of me," he said. "And when you were singing I was proud of you, so that's why I was sad."

LET'S SEE IF HE'S READY TO FIGHT

Most nights we prayed for Daddy together. The boys would listen to my prayer first, then say a similar one with their own twist.

"Dear Lord," Brandon said as we all sat on his bed. "I pray for my Daddy. Please keep him safe, and that no bad guys get him. And I hope I'll see Daddy again and I hope Mami and Daddy will be friends. And thank you for my TV, and my Tyler, and the moon sky and the sun sky and my toys. Amen."

⌒⌒

"God can do that for us," I'd remind them after we'd all pray. After everything God had done in my life so far, I believed he could.

At the end of the summer I got a call from my mother-in-law.

"I'm going to pick up the boys this weekend," she said. "And Gavin wants to pick them up from me on Saturday."

As much faith as I had that he'd one day be back, the call itself shocked me.

"Really?" I asked.

"Yes," she said. "God is good!"

As much as I'd wanted this moment to happen for the boys, as much as I'd prayed for this day, I suddenly felt resentment.

"Oh," I said to myself, beginning to seethe. "Suddenly you just feel like seeing them again after a whole year of hurting them with your absence, and it just gets to happen for you?" Part of me wanted to say no. Maybe I should just tell him he doesn't get to just walk in and out of their lives. Maybe he needs to fight me in court for the privilege of seeing them. Because that's what it is, a privilege! Let's see how badly he wants to have them back in his life. Let's see if he's ready to fight for it!

But when Friday came, I walked them down to Evelyn's car. I waved good-bye as they drove away, then went upstairs and broke down.

WEDDING ALBUM

On a Sunday afternoon after church, I decided to give my home a deep cleaning. As always, my full-time work schedule and responsibilities with the boys consumed me, often leaving my apartment in disarray as housework took a backseat to more important issues. The boys helped me as we swept and mopped our floors, cleaned and organized toys, polished the bathroom, and gutted closets to sort through, purge, and rearrange. My wedding album sat in one of the piles and the boys found it, curiously opening its pages. I sat with them waiting for the conversation and questions to come. I waited for Tyler especially, since he had been too young when Gavin left to remember a time so different from now. For most of his life his father and I barely spoke. And now he was looking at pictures where the two of us were kissing and holding each other lovingly on our wedding day.

Gavin had been back in their lives for a few months now, but I never saw him. Evelyn would pick up the boys from my place, and Gavin would pick them up from hers.

"You were kissing Daddy," Tyler said with a giggle.

"Yes," I said smiling at him, "I was."

They beamed with each page, looking at the two of us together. They laughed at their cousins, who were so young in the photographs.

"I wish Daddy lived with us," Brandon said. "But he can't because you're not friends anymore, right?"

"Do you hate Daddy?" Tyler chimed in.

"No," I said. "Of course I don't hate Daddy."

I spoke as we continued to go through the album.

"Daddy and I were best friends, and then we got married. We loved each other very much. And one day, we stopped being friends. I don't really know how that happened, and it made me sad, but I'm okay now. I can never hate Daddy, because he gave me you guys. And you are the best part of my life."

It made no sense that we weren't speaking. It seemed unreal that it was over a year since I'd even seen him. But that was the reality, and I didn't know how to explain it in a way that made sense to the boys. Whenever they fought, I taught them the importance of forgiveness and making up. And yet the two most important people in their lives couldn't do that with each other.

"We're not friends now," I continued. "But I'm just going to keep praying that one day we will be. God answered your prayer to see Daddy again, right? I think one day God will help us to be friends." They seemed satisfied with that, then ran off to finish sponging the giant blackboard in their room. I continued to look at the pictures. The sting of pain I might have felt years ago wasn't there.

The flood of memories made me happy. I remembered the dance with my father, resting my cheek on his shoulder, and feeling all of his love for me in his embrace. As I remembered, I felt grateful for my wedding day. I got to experience my father walking me down the aisle, I was able to see and feel the love and support of so many who continued to give me their love and support. It was a fun day, and it was a celebration of love in so many ways. And as justified as I felt at times to be angry or to despise Gavin, that wasn't what I felt now. He was a big part of my life. There were great times when we were friends and some wonderful moments in our marriage. And, of course, he gave me the best part of my life: my two beautiful boys. There's no room for hate there.

GO HUG MOM

I was irritable that morning. The boys were under my skin as I tried to get them ready for school. They played when they should have been getting dressed, had a sword fight with their toothbrushes instead of brushing their teeth, and dragged through breakfast time as they talked more than they chewed.

Tyler was in kindergarten now, and Brandon in first grade. Every time we were late, I'd get a call that evening, an annoying prerecorded message informing me of what I already knew: "Hello this is to inform you that your child arrived late for school today. It is important for your child to arrive at school on time for instruction. Please keep in mind that your child is required by the chancellor of New York City to have ninety percent attendance for promotion. So please send your child to school on time every day. Thank you, good-bye."

After that call, I'd get an identical call for Tyler. Before the school year began, we'd spent the month in Florida as usual. It was always a hard time adjusting back to the grind of work, subways, kids, housework, and everything else. But this time I couldn't shake the gloom of going back to my hectic schedule. I was burned out and couldn't wrap my head around keeping this up for years to come.

"Hurry up!" I shouted as they fumbled with their shoes.

"Let's go!" I nagged as they put on their jackets. "You're going to make us late!"

I mumbled under my breath as we walked to the elevator then slushed through the gray, winter morning to school. I couldn't wait to get there. I needed to be child-free, and the sooner we got there the sooner that would happen.

"Okay, get in. Bye," I said when we arrived. I shooed them through the gate to the entrance door without my customary kiss-and-hug. Brandon got to the door, but then turned back to give me a quick embrace. I stood there waiting for them to walk through the door, but Brandon stopped Tyler in his tracks and started whispering in his ear.

"What are you doing?" I barked. "You're late! Get inside!"

Tyler walked toward me with that "obedient little brother" mug on his face, and then I realized what Brandon was telling him to do. "Go hug Mom."

My heart crumbled with guilt. I didn't deserve their hugs or my Brandon's compassion that day.

Tyler wrapped his arms around me, covering my guilt with love.

THIS DOESN'T HAVE TO BE MY LIFE

I sat there numb, caught off guard by what Brandon's teachers were telling me.

"We think it would be better to remove him from the Dual-French program," they repeated. Brandon was unfocused in class, caught up in the world of daydreams, and uninterested in his lessons at school.

But I wasn't going to allow him to be removed.

"It's my fault," I tried to explain. "I get home late from work and I don't have a lot of time to help him with homework. But I'll do better." The truth was that I did make the time, but it was rushed, and it ended in both of us becoming frustrated and angry. After a long day of school and an after-school they didn't enjoy, the last thing either of them wanted to do was sit down and do homework.

"We don't have fun in after-school," Brandon would argue. "I want to play when we get home." I knew he was right. It was a terrible after-school program that did little to engage the kids. But it was free. The other after-schools were ridiculously expensive.

"I don't want to do homework with you, either. There are lots of other things I have to do!" I'd yell back. "But we have to do this." It was true. I hated doing homework with him, because after a long day at work and an hour-long subway commute home, I was exhausted. And even without the homework, there were still a hundred other things around the house that demanded my attention before the bath, reading, and bedtime routine. I was drowning, and I didn't know how to change that.

⌒

"I spend most of my time helping other kids with their homework and I don't even have the time to properly help my son, who is struggling," I said, venting about how overwhelmed I was by my life.

"That's just the life of a single mother," my friend responded matter-of-factly.

She was a single mother, too, and knew the struggle all too well. But her answer did not sit well with me. It had no hope or choices.

"No!" I argued. "This doesn't have to be my life!"

I loved my job, and I knew that God had placed me there for a purpose. But now, more than ever, I knew my season at Graffiti was over.

"How will you live if you quit?" My sister asked me, concerned when I told her what I was going to do.

"I have savings," I said, "and I should be getting a good amount on my tax return this year. Then I can write and pray for a contract."

"What if it doesn't work out?" she asked. "That's a scary step to make with no guarantees."

"I can't think about failure," I said. "And anyway, it can't be scarier than the stress I'm living in now. I'm no good to my kids if I'm always feeling overwhelmed."

A week later I gave my notice as children's director at Graffiti Church.

Pastor Taylor graciously celebrated the work I'd done for the church and community. With encouragement and a beautiful prayer, he affirmed that it was time for me to become the writer, the artist, and the mother God made me to be.

TYLER'S SURGERY

The monster tonsils had to go. I helped Tyler put on the tiger-print hospital pajamas, then watched him play in the colorful waiting room filled with toys.

I was nervous—not just because my son was about to have surgery, but because Gavin would be there. The boys had been seeing him for months now through Evelyn, but it was the first time I would see him in over a year.

"Daddy!"

Tyler ran into his arms and Gavin picked him up.

He nodded toward me.

"Hi."

"Hi."

I quietly watched them play on Gavin 's iPad.

"How long did they say he'd be in surgery?" Gavin asked.

"About an hour, maybe less," I responded.

Communication. That first small exchange of words felt enormous.

"You can follow me," the nurse said. "We're ready."

We walked down the corridor just as my parents arrived.

"Oh, good. We made it," my mother said, breathless. They both hugged and kissed Tyler as we continued to follow the nurse.

"You can all wait here," said the nurse. "Mom, follow me."

I carried Tyler into the operating room, laid him on the table, and waited until he stopped giggling under the anesthesia mask.

Back in the waiting room, Evelyn had arrived. To my surprise, Gavin was engaged in polite small talk with my parents. A scene that I would have imagined being extremely uncomfortable suddenly felt right.

Less than hour later, the nurse came back in.

"Mom and Dad, you can go see your son now. He's waking up from the anesthesia."

Mom and Dad—I had not heard or even thought about those two small words put together in a long time.

⌣

Tyler was delirious with pain.

"I can't breathe!" he yelled. "I can't breathe!"

The two of us reached out to comfort him. He continued to cry. I climbed into his bed to hold him. He squirmed and wriggled in pain. "I can't breathe," he continued to say. I began to panic.

"Maybe we should call the nurse over," I said.

Gavin reached out for him and I passed Tyler over to sit on his father's lap.

"Tyler, you're okay," he said calmly.

"But I can't breathe!" he screamed.

"You can breathe," he said gently. "If you can cry, that means you can breathe. You see that machine over there?" Tyler looked. "That says your breathing is okay."

The nurse brought a cup of ice chips over. Gavin fed them to Tyler as he continued to talk him down from hysteria. I was relieved someone else could be calm and strong for Tyler, especially since watching him in so much pain was making me anxious. For once I didn't have to find the strength out of nowhere. I sat there and watched Gavin comfort our son. Not my son. Ours.

CLIMBING

C limbing," Brandon said as he looked up at the rock-climbing wall stretching sixty feet above his head.

"Climb on," I responded, letting him know I was ready as well.

After years of watching my boys climb everything, I'd found a sport that gave them full permission to climb walls.

"Take!" he yelled, letting me know to hold tight as he let go of the wall to hang in midair. He shook out his arms and looked at the wall to plan out his next move.

My friend Erica watched him climb for the first time and looked at me with a mix of amazement and fear. "Aren't you afraid for him, going up that high?"

"No" I said, "because I control the rope that holds him. I know he's okay."

She shook her head, still baffled.

"But he's so high! How is he not afraid?"

I looked at my little boy dangling sixty feet over my head.

"Because he knows I would never let him fall."

LAST STAFF MEETING

I sprinkled the large round table in the meeting room with feathers and filled each plate with snacks that represented my theme. I had made angel-wing bookmarks for each place setting with Psalm 91:4: *He will cover you with his feathers. He will shelter you with his wings. His faithful promises are your armor and protection.*

This would be my last time leading the staff meeting before my last day at work. My first had been French themed, with Edith Piaf singing in the background, a lace table cloth covered with croissants, creamy French yogurt, caramel tea (the tea I used to drink in France), Nutella, and other delicious goodies. I loved creating an atmosphere and pulling together themes to go with my devotion. I was going to miss that.

"Wow," my co-workers said as they walked in and sat around the table, looking at the goodies and reading their bookmarks.

After we ate a bit and chatted, I presented my devotion.

"As you can see, my theme is wings," I said. I read the verse on the cards and spoke about the way a mother bird protects her babies under her wing. "I know God sent me here to you for that protection. When I came here, I arrived like a broken bird who couldn't fly. And with your love and care, and incredible confidence in who I could be, I became stronger, and my heart was healed." I stopped, realizing I should be crying but I wasn't.

"You see, I'm not even crying right now." I laughed. "My first year here, I couldn't get through prayer requests without bursting into tears! But I'm stronger now, and you're a big part of that."

I knew I was ready to fly away and, even though I had no idea what God had in store for me next, I couldn't wait to see what it was.

SOMETHING NEW

I waited in the school yard with other parents at 2:50 p.m. as teachers led their classes out for dismissal. Brandon came out, daydreaming in line as he followed his classmates. He didn't have to follow after-school workers to bring him to another building or wait in boredom for me to walk through the door after dark. The sun was bright as I stood there, waiting for him to see me, and when he did, his face beamed even brighter. "Mami!" he yelled, raising his hand for the teacher to shake it and release him to me. He ran to me and I picked him up in my arms. The other parents said hello to their children, but no one could have possibly been more excited than I was that afternoon. Tyler came out next, and he didn't even wait for his teacher to dismiss him before he came running over to us. This simple act of picking up my children from school was monumental for me. I could let them play in the snow with their friends, bring them home for hot chocolate and cookies. I could sign them up for karate classes and whatever else they wanted to do after school. I could sit with them calmly and help them with their homework, unrushed. Nothing else would press me for my attention when I was with them. The house would already be clean, the dishes washed, the laundry done, the dinner prepped. As I stood there embracing my boys, who were thrilled to see me, I knew I had made the right decision in leaving Graffiti. And I also knew I had to fight to keep it this way. The savings would last only so long, and I had to get busy while they were in school.

᭺

Every day I worked on manuscripts and proposals. I knew my writing and getting published again would be my main ticket to maintaining the life I wanted to live with my children. But until that happened, I needed to bring in money in other ways. I promoted my music playgroup classes and birthday parties. I painted a mural for the church I grew up in on the Lower East Side. A pastry chef friend taught me how to make fondant and sculpt cakes so I could master another medium to create art. I continued to record my music in a friend's music studio, and I wrote new songs on my piano and guitar. I made a goal to perform every month and share my story through music and words.

⌒

I understood God's call in my life to sing about my pain and victories. Music had been a part of my healing for so many years, but now I also got to see how the music helped others as well. After my first café performance after leaving my job, a woman came up to me with tears in her eyes. "Thank you," she said. "Thank you for opening your heart to us." She was going through a similar struggle, and the words, the music, and the testimony of healing gave her hope. More women came, more tears, and men, too, thanking me for a word of encouragement they needed to hear. It was such a blessing to know that, beyond my own healing, God was using the brokenness of my past and the talents he'd given me to help heal others as well.

A TICKET TO FRANCE

O h, it's from Anaïs!" I squealed, opening the envelope sent from Lyon, France.

⌒

Years before, when I still lived with my parents, I had met Remi Rochette. He was a sweet, funny, and soft-spoken college student from France who melted my family's heart. When he returned to France after his studies, he asked if his sister could stay with us for a visit to

New York City. Anaïs was eighteen years old, tall, and beautiful. To my parents' surprise, she spoke Spanish, too, and we enjoyed having her with us. For three weeks that summer I showed her every nook and cranny of my city: the World Trade Center, Chinatown, Central Park, the Apollo Theater, and Yankee Stadium, to name a few. Years later, I applied to work in France as a teacher's assistant. I couldn't choose where I worked or lived, but, to my shock and elation, the school chosen for me was down the street from Anaïs's apartment!

She helped me settle into the town. We ate together, went to the movies, even found a gymnastics center where we bounced on trampolines and took tumbling classes every week. Every weekend we drove to her parents' house in the country, where they embraced me as their own.

My first Christmas without my family was with them. I sat with them around a huge wooden table at their grandmother's house and enjoyed a feast near a cozy fireplace. They took me skiing and on vacation to see castles in the Loire Valley. For a year I was part of the family. I was crushed to leave, but we kept in touch. I returned a year later with my sister for two weeks; she and my French family fell in love with each other, too. There had been visits from Anaïs and her brothers to New York City, and they even met up with my sister in Italy when she was on vacation.

⌒

I opened the envelope with anticipation. Anaïs just had her first child, and I was hoping it was a picture of baby Eloise. But instead it was an invitation to her wedding in France.

Impossible, would have been my reaction just months before. But nothing seemed impossible anymore. I looked up flights, and found a great price! Of course I had to fly into Istanbul first and the trip would take sixteen hours, but I didn't care. Next I called my friend Danielle and my mother-in-law to see if it was at all possible for them to watch the boys if I went. They said yes!

I would be dipping into my savings, the savings I had just begun to live on after quitting my job. The careful, fearful, sensible part of me would have said no way. But something new overshadowed those feelings; my long-ago carefree spirit, my newfound hope and sense of adventure ignited inside of me. After a few clicks on my computer and a joyful dance around my living room, I was on my way to France.

THE WEDDING

It was a beautiful day, perfect for a wedding. The 800-year-old church was perched on top of a hill like a fairy tale. Its pale stone façade showed no sign of age or injury—just strength and grace.

This was really happening. I was in France. I looked over the hill at the French countryside with its lush greens, wildflowers, and ancient cottages tucked in between. The bells began to ring as Anaïs appeared in her wedding gown. She was breathtaking, her carefree smile showing no signs of hesitation or fear. I joined the others inside the dim, candlelit sanctuary as the ceremony began. I stood in front as Anaïs had requested and dedicated a song that I wrote for the bride and groom. It was a prayer for her marriage.

I pray that kindness would live with you always,
And understanding would follow you everywhere.
I pray your love for each other would grow and grow,
And nothing in this world would ever take it away.

This is my prayer for you,
that you would walk with one another forever.
This is my prayer for you,

That these promises stay true beyond I do.

This is my prayer.

Anaïs and her new husband smiled at me as I sang. They looked happy.

⌒

I remembered Gavin and me on our wedding day, how my cousin's wife had smiled at us. I knew her marriage was struggling. I'd smiled back, knowing her heart was breaking as she perhaps recalled her own wedding and wondered where it all went wrong.

⌒

I continued to sing about patience and kindness. I sang about making the choice to stand together through the pain and strife that life will surely bring. I understood more than ever that true love is a choice. It begins with a feeling, but it can only survive by choosing that person every day, even when those feelings of love begin to fade.

⌒

It's easy to say Gavin didn't choose me, but I didn't choose him, either. I chose myself. I focused on my own struggles and all I felt he was doing to make me unhappy in our marriage. I didn't make an effort to understand who he was, because I was too preoccupied with who he wasn't. I didn't choose to fight for our marriage; instead I tip-toed around it, hoping it would get better by itself, like a timid little mouse. We made lots of choices in and out of our marriage, but neither of us chose to truly love.

And now all we can do is forgive each other for our choices and hope to make better ones for our children.

⌒⌒

At the end of the wedding, as the bride and groom walked away from the altar, I led a small choir through "Oh Happy Day." I sang into the microphone and clapped my hands, encouraging the congregation to stand up and do the same. To the shock of many, everyone did.

The family later told me that this was the first time they'd ever seen the congregation respond in such a way. "Catholic churches in France, especially in the countryside, don't stand up and clap to music," said Anaïs's uncle as we walked toward the cars to the reception. Congregations in that region were known to be very somber and quiet.

"Yes." Her brother Hubert laughed in agreement. "As old as this church is, I think you just made history."

⌒⌒

The reception was in a sixteenth-century chateau, its façade laced in delicate climbing vines. After a cocktail hour outside featuring French wine, tasty hors d'oeuvres, and cotton candy, which I was to find out later was meant for the children—after I ate two—we went inside to celebrate some more. I felt beautiful in my red dress, the one I'd exercised and fasted for weeks to fit into. I would make up for all my dieting that night, eating every dish that was set before me. The dessert table, with every confectionary imaginable, was presented with grand sparklers shooting out as we clapped to the music. The bride and groom poured bottles of champagne atop the pyramid of champagne glasses, filling each one as it cascaded down. I danced with my French family and ate; then I danced and ate some more. By 4 a.m. I had retreated to my room, but everyone else continued to celebrate until the sun came up. The next day we ate some more and played games outside on the grounds. The beauty inspired me to photograph everything and everyone. I wanted to capture every moment and never forget how I felt in this magical place.

～～

I spent the next few days with the family. I felt at home again, as if I had never left. That was how I felt every day—as if I had never left France and my life in New York City and everything that had happened in the last few years was the dream. Anaïs took me to visit Saint-Étienne, our old town where we lived years ago. And, as marvelous as this trip already was, Remi and Hubert surprised me with a trip to the French Alps. We were off to ski in the snowcapped mountains of Flaine.

YOU'RE IMPORTANT, TOO

I was surrounded by peaks of white, and as I skied down, it was as if I were floating in heaven. It was cold enough to ski in the morning, but by afternoon it was warm enough to swim.

Hubert and Remi decided to ski some more while I enjoyed the outdoor pool completely alone. I leaned back in the water, looking at the majesty that surrounded me. I listened to the quiet rippling of the water and gloried in the landscape of snowy mountains towering above.

I was living a moment that had seemed impossible not so long ago.

After years of heartache, struggle, responsibility, and fatigue, I'd assumed my life of adventure was a thing of the past. As a single mom I had had to sacrifice my own needs and wants for the love of my boys. Yet that day, surrounded by his glory, I felt God softly whispering,

"You're important, too, Karen." I realized how much I'd needed to know that I matter, that I'm cared for, and that there's so much more to look forward to.

My trip was almost over. In a few days I would see my beautiful boys again. I couldn't wait to show them all I'd experienced. One day, I was going to bring them here, to experience it for themselves.

⌣

As I boarded the plane to fly home days later, I wasn't sad to say good-bye. This was not the end. This was just the beginning.

READING GROUP GUIDE

NEWLYWED

1. How does your experience with pre-wedding jitters—your own or brides and grooms you know—compare to Karen's and Gavin's?

2. What do you feel Karen should have done differently while dating?

3. How did Karen's experience on dating outside of her faith affect you?

4. What would you have said to Karen about "purity"?

5. When Gavin said "Your faith was bendable," how would you have responded?

6. What stood out for you the most about marriage in this section? Why?

EXPECTANT MOM

1. Which of Karen's pre-birth feelings have you or women you know experienced?

2. Karen enjoyed being pampered by her mom during her pregnancy. What are some ways you can lighten an expectant mother's burden?

3. How was Karen's pregnancy like or unlike pregnancies of women you know who delayed motherhood until the mid-thirties?

4. What most stood out for you about pregnancy in this section? Why?

NEW MOM

1. How did the new baby both strengthen and divide the new parents' relationship? Was their experience similar or dissimilar to yours or couples you know?

2. What do you think about Gavin's words "Not everyone loves like you"?

3. Must a husband and wife lose the relationship they had while dating?

4. What did you note Karen and Gavin did not do after their child was born that contributed to their distance?

5. What in this section stood out for you the most about first-time parenting and how men and women parent differently? Why?

MOTHER OF TWO

1. Is Karen's perception that mothering a second child will take away from her firstborn justified?

2. Are the feelings she has after she gives birth similar to feelings experienced by you or women you know?

3. What did you think about Karen comparing her relationship with someone else's in "Love in Chinese"?

4. Who in your life was like Karen's aunt who prepared her for difficulties in life?

5. What in this section stood out for you the most about motherhood? Why?

SINGLE MOM

1. How does Karen's experience compare to what you have learned in relating to moms going through divorce or separation?

2. What did you identify with most in this chapter?

3. As you read the chapter where Karen contemplated something drastic and harmful to alleviate her pain, were you reminded of destructive thoughts you may have contemplated in the midst of grief? If so, what made you change your mind?

4. Has God ever used someone unexpected to tell you you're going to be okay, similar to when Karen's little boy snaps her out of her panic?

5. What stood out for you the most about single motherhood in this section? Why?

HEALING

1. In what ways did Graffiti Church, the Mission Teams, and Pastor Taylor work toward Karen's healing?

2. In what ways did Graffiti Church, the Mission Teams and Pastor Taylor work *unknowingly* toward Karen's healing?

3. Is there something specifically crafted in you that has helped or may help someone grieving?

4. Blessings seemed to fall into place on Karen's journey to healing. What blessing came your way after grief, and how did it shift your perception of God?

5. Karen was inspired to push herself because of Pastor Taylor's belief that she could. Describe a situation in which a pastor allowed you to see your full potential.

6. For Karen, a main source of healing was in singing. How has Christian music helped you heal?

7. What stood out for you the most in this section? Why?

THE MOTHER GOD MADE ME TO BE

1. What do you feel you are not doing well with your children?

2. Where is God in the balance of your shortcomings and working toward the best for your children?

3. Why do you think Karen had a change of heart after Gavin first returned to the boys' life? Were her feelings valid?

4. Pastor Taylor gave Karen guidance and advice as she worked toward healing. Which words of wisdom from Pastor Taylor were most impactful?

5. Karen made a bold decision for her and her boys with no promise of success. Do you view her move as foolish or inspiring?

6. What stood out for you the most in this section? Why?